WHEN LINCOLN DIED

WHEN LINCOLN DIED

BY RALPH BORRESON

APPLETON-CENTURY
New York

To Ann

First edition

APPLETON-CENTURY
AFFILIATE OF
MEREDITH PRESS

Library of Congress Catalog Card Number: 65-21679

MANUFACTURED IN THE UNITED STATES OF AMERICA FOR MEREDITH PRESS

VAN REES PRESS • NEW YORK

INTRODUCTION

BY HENRY STEELE COMMAGER

The American Civil War began with one and acquired a second major objective, and achieved both of them. The first was to save the Union, and Lincoln made clear the nature of that priority in his famous letter to Horace Greeley. The second, originally subordinate to the first, but eventually of equal dignity, was to free the slaves. Both of these war aims were vindicated—that is rare in history.

It has often been observed that these two objectives were achieved in ways which partly defeated their original purpose, or that, whatever the achievement, the cost was intolerably high. To the first of these objections it might be answered that no end in history is ever realized quite as it was first envisioned, and that, in the words of Euripides,

> The end men looked for cometh not
> And a path there was where no man thought
> So hath it fallen here.

And as for the second objection, we might reply, in the words of Lincoln's Second Inaugural address:

> If God wills that it [the war] continue until all the wealth piled up by the bondsman's two hundred and fifty years of unrequited toil shall be sunk, and until every drop of blood drawn by the lash shall be paid by another drawn by the sword, as was said three thousand years ago, so still it must be said, "The Judgments of the Lord are true and righteous altogether."

There is, perhaps, a less poetic answer to both objections, one rooted, if not in history, then in experience: that whatever the cost of preserving the Union and freeing the slaves, there was no other way of achieving these ends except by war and violence, and that, in a sense, to quarrel with the result is to quarrel with the objectives. Certainly, while there is reason to believe that statesmanship might have avoided the war, there is no reason to suppose that once secession was a reality, the Union could have been cemented together again except by force. Nor is there any persuasive reason to believe that Southerners, who were willing to fight and die for slavery, would have surrendered it voluntarily; the notion that slavery was, somehow, on the way out, is one born of sentiment, not reason. We should not forget that as late as 1865 the little State of Delaware, with only three thousand slaves, yet rejected the Thirteenth Amendment.

No doubt about it, the cost was high—the cost of the war, the cost of Reconstruction. We have long been familiar with the story of Reconstruction, and even the most intransigent, North and South alike, are ready to admit now that the thing was managed badly. The Union was reconstructed, but it is something of an exaggeration to say that the South was; clearly, the process left lasting scars. We have perhaps been less aware of, or less sensitive to, the failure of the reconstruction process for the Negro, who was allowed to shift for himself, and in the end abandoned to the mercies of his former masters who showed little mercy, and who was cheated out of that equality solemnly guaranteed in the Constitution. Now, a century later, we are called upon to take up this unfinished business, to overcome Southern bitterness and intransigence and lawlessness, and make good on promises neglected for almost a century.

Would it all have been different had Lincoln lived?

It is the death of Lincoln we are called upon to consider by this collection of literary and pictorial source material, rather than the life. But the life and death are part of a single pattern, however convulsive the transition may seem. It was the hatreds engendered by the war that erupted in the assassination of Lincoln; it was the passion for revenge engenderd by the assassination that exacerbated the processes of Reconstruction.

Would the history of Reconstruction, would the fate of the Negro, have been different had Lincoln lived?

We are in the realm here of speculation, but not of mere speculation, for Lincoln is not an unknown quantity, nor are his purposes and his program. From the very beginning of the conflict he had thought about the Reconstruction of the Union and about the Southern Negro, and he had formulated most of those principles which he hoped would govern the postwar years.

Lincoln was just, moderate, and firm. He had one paramount object: to save and restore the Union; and he was deeply impatient with all theories, doctrines, and arguments which threatened to distract him from that object, even with the arguments of constitutional law. It was characteristic that when Secretary Seward reminded him of some constitutional precedent from the reign of Charles I, he observed that all he remembered of Charles I was that he had lost his head! Lincoln rejected, therefore, speculation about the constitutional position of the seceded States—whether they were "conquered territory," whether they had "forfeited" their rights as States, "is bad as a basis of controversy and good for nothing at all—a merely pernicious abstraction." As for the seceded States "finding themselves safely at home, it would be utterly immaterial whether they had ever been abroad." Lincoln set forth his own plan for Reconstruction in a series of state papers, speeches and letters. It was eminently practical and commonsensical. It envisioned getting the machinery of state and national government functioning once more. And as for punishing those who had participated in the rebellion, there was to be none of that. Let the leaders escape; the guilt of the others could be wiped away by the "King's Cure"—the Presidential pardon. Lincoln wanted no more violence, no more bloodshed; there had been enough of that.

Would Lincoln have been able to impose his will on the Congressional Radicals? That we do not know. But during the four years of the war he had proved himself more subtle, more resourceful, and more powerful, than his opponents. He had imposed his will on his Cabinet—on the shrewd Seward, who wanted to take over the Presidency; on the ambitious Chase, who was ever contriving and plotting for the succession; on the arrogant Stanton, who made so much trouble for poor Andrew Johnson. He had imposed his will on the Congress, partly by outwitting it, as in his failure to call a special session until midsummer, 1861, and partly by the skillful deployment of patronage and politics. He had, in the end, imposed his will on his generals—something Jefferson Davis was never able to do. McClellan, who thought that he was both wiser and stronger than the President, learned that he was neither, and the greatest of Union generals, U. S. Grant, worked harmoniously with his Commander-in-Chief. And Lincoln had even imposed, if not his will, then his purpose, on the governments of Britain and France, conducting his diplomacy (and the war) with such skill that notwithstanding ardent sympathy for the Confederacy on the part of the upper classes, neither nation dared intervene in the blockade or recognize the South.

There is an additional reason to suppose that Lincoln might have had his way with Reconstruction. For Lincoln's death revealed a reservoir of affection and devotion which—had he lived to draw upon it—might have been irresistible. By the spring of 1865 Lincoln was the man who had saved the Union when all seemed desperate; he was the Great Emancipator; he was Father Abraham. In a way which few of his peers realized or understood he had caught the imagination of the people of his country. Whitman's last moving elegy was right:

> The ship has weather'd every rack, the prize we sought is won,
> The port is near, the bells I hear, the people all exulting. . . .

With the immense prestige of victory, with the matchless hold on the affections of the masses of the people, the devotion of the freedmen, the confidence, even, of the leaders of the South—with all this Lincoln might have been strong enough to direct and control the processes of Reconstruction, to guide them along the channels of moderation, and to avoid some of the misunderstanding and bitterness and frustrations that attended that chapter of our history.

What of the second objective—freedom and equality for the Negro slave? Is there any reason to suppose that, had he lived, Lincoln might have hastened progress toward these beneficent ends?

Here the temptation to speculate is more seductive and more dangerous. For if the assassination gave the Radicals an excuse to impose harsher terms upon the defeated South than might otherwise have been possible, did it not impel them, at the same time, to a more generous and more sympathetic championship of the Negro? Certainly it should have done so. It was the Radicals, after all, who pushed through the Fourteenth and Fifteenth Amendments, the Freedmen's Bureau Bill, the Civil Rights Act, and a series of Reconstruction Acts and Force Acts looking to—or at least squinting at—a broader area of freedom for the Negro. All this, one might suppose, augured well for the vindication of the second war aim: freedom and equality for the Blacks. Yet Radical zeal for the freedmen, sincere though it doubtless was, did not have staying power. Lincoln had hoped to educate the Southern Negro to his new political responsibilities, and the Southern white to Negro political equality, gradually and painlessly, to insinuate equality into the fabric of Southern life and thought, as it were. This was the policy he proposed in Louisiana and Tennessee; it was doubtless the policy he would have supported everywhere in the South in the postwar years, had he lived.

But the idealism of the antislavery movement, and of the war itself, petered out, the North became tired of the "Southern question" which was, of course, the Negro question; the Radicals themselves came to prefer order and stability, particularly in the political and economic realms, to continual turmoil, and thus notified the South that it could have its way only if it indulged in continual turmoil! Within a decade or so of the death of the Great Emancipator, "white supremacy," euphemistically called "home rule," was re-established in the South, at the expense, of course, of the Negro.

Would Lincoln's policy of moderation have proved more successful in overcoming Southern intransigence? That we will never know. But we may venture the opinion that it could scarcely have been less successful.

These are some of the considerations that occur to us as we contemplate the death of Lincoln, just a century ago. There are others. There is, for example, the spectacle of violence. The record presented in this series of pictures is a somber one, from the murder of Lincoln by the mad John Wilkes Booth to the judicial murder of Mrs. Surratt by a military commission whose very authority was dubious. We are accustomed, now, to violence, and, alas, not unaccustomed to assassination, but Lincoln was the first President to fall to an assassin, and the first prominent public figure since Alexander Hamilton to die by violence. Because he was the first, the shock of his death was cataclysmic. Americans had thought, somehow, that they were exempt from such things, here in the New World, but discovered that they were not. It was part of the end of innocence, not of real but of imagined innocence.

Then there is the spectacle of myths in the making. Lloyd Lewis has conjured up for us many of these "Myths after Lincoln." Lincoln lent himself, almost irresistibly, to the process. His origins humble and even mysterious, his youth gentle and simple, his speech pithy and wise, his manner benign, he emerged briefly to save his people and free the slaves, and died as the lilacs bloomed. We catch a glimpse here, too, of the beginnings of some of those other myths that gathered around the hapless John Wilkes Booth, dark hints of complicity in high places, all easy enough to understand against the lurid background of conspiracy and war, the curious mixture of truth and fancy, of history and rumor and imagination, that was soon to come to the surface.

Mr. Borreson has given us here a detailed and faithful record of the death of Lincoln, a comprehensive collection of source materials, partly literary but mostly photographic, that permits us to follow the phantasmagoric events of those desperate days with an intimacy denied most of those who lived through them.

CONTENTS

FOREWORD

This book was begun many years ago. The motivating force was the one which impelled Leigh-Mallory to climb his mountain—it was there. The mountain, in this case sometimes as literal as it was figurative, was what appeared to be the need to tell the story of Lincoln's death in the words of his people. Some aspects of the book's preparation may be of interest.

Demanding in terms of time and effort was selecting, from an amazing plethora of sources, the precise quotation to convey the narrative at given points as the tale developed. The seemingly endless task of correlating the components, picture, quotation, chronology, story and space all simultaneously, was frequently frustrating and always time consuming. The pursuit of illustrations was both baffling and rewarding. All the principal depositories were visited and countless letters written, often futilely, but occasionally with the delightful result of turning up a prize.

In a work of this nature help from others is imperative. Through the years of preparation expert aid has come from many places and many persons. It is not possible to list all of these here—most have had my thanks—but some cannot in conscience be omitted.

Among the scores who have helped the name of one stands out. This is Miss Margaret A. Flint of the Illinois State Historical Library, whose gracious assistance for years has been of incalculable value and who is so eminently deserving of this special expression of heartfelt gratitude.

There is indebtedness felt for the kindness of Maurice J. Baker in making available the reminiscences and photograph of his grandfather, Lieut. Luther B. Baker. Most helpful, too, were Dr. Richard D. Mudd, who permitted use of a rare picture relating to his grandfather, Dr. Samuel A. Mudd, and Daniel W. Jones, NBC, who gave technical advice. Making their expert knowledge freely available were Miss Josephine Cobb, National Archives; R. Gerald McMurtry, Lincoln National Life Foundation; Cornelius W. Heine, National Park Service; Miss Virginia Daiker and Carl Stange, Library of Congress; Miss Betty Ezequelle, New York Historical Society. For services rendered, a special word of thanks to Frank E. Morse for a memorable pursuit of Booth from Ford's to Garrett's farm, and to Peter Weed of the publisher's staff, who with consummate tact blended easy cajolery with mild intimidation to keep the project afloat.

But as Lincoln might have said, "It is to the dead that we owe the greater debt." For it is in the words of those who lived a century ago that this work takes validity and form. To all of these, nearly sevenscore, ministers and murderers, lawyers and liars, clerks and cabinet officers, poltroons and heroes, jurists and journalists, dressmakers and actresses, privates and generals, literary lights and literary hacks, solons and saloon keepers, a resounding word of thanks. And to the dozens of artists and photographers, nameless now, a very special salute for their indispensable contributions.

Sheldon, Iowa R. B.

CHAPTER I

O MOODY, TEARFUL NIGHT!

ASSASSINATION

ILLINOIS STATE HISTORICAL LIBRARY

The President's Carriage

CHICAGO HISTORICAL SOCIETY

Henry R. Rathbone, Brevet Major in the Army of the United States, being duly sworn, says that on the 14th day of April, instant, at about twenty minutes past eight o'clock in the evening, he, with Miss Clara H. Harris, left his residence at the corner of Fifteenth and H Streets, and joined the President and Mrs. Lincoln and went with them in their carriage to Ford's Theatre in Tenth Street.

It was a little after nine o'clock, and I was in the lobby handing out my programs, when the presidential party arrived. There were but four—the President, Mrs. Lincoln, Miss Clara Harris, the daughter of Senator Ira Harris of New York, and her fiancé, Major Henry R. Rathbone. I was in doubt whether to hand Mr. Lincoln a program or not, but he smiled at me, nodded and said something in an aside to Mrs. Lincoln, and held out his hand. I stepped forward and gave each member of the party one of my printed sheets. Mrs. Lincoln looked at me, too, and gave me a smile. They passed within the theater.

JOSEPH HAZLETON,
program boy at Ford's.

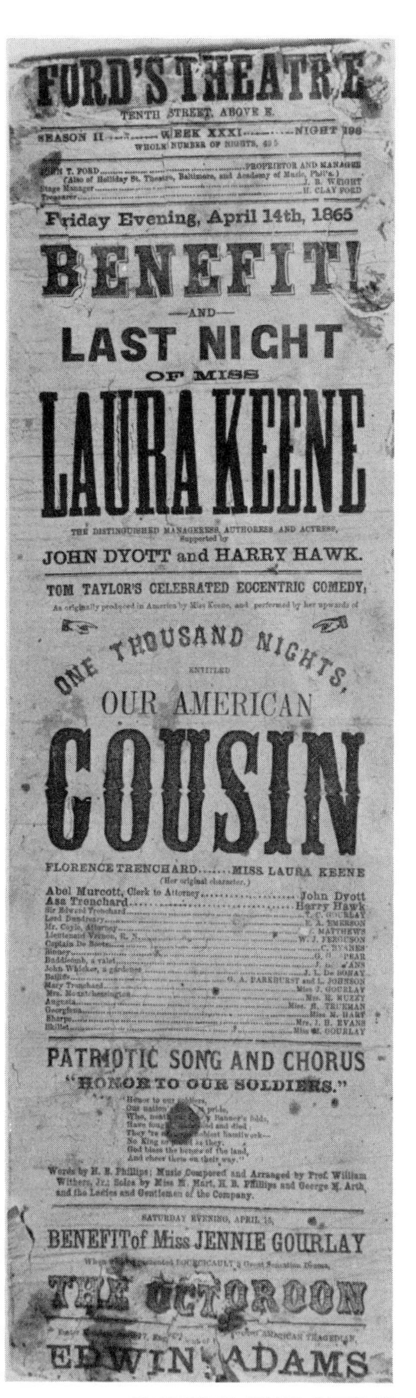
FORD'S THEATRE
TENTH STREET, ABOVE E.
SEASON II ... WEEK XXXI ... NIGHT 196
WHOLE NUMBER OF NIGHTS, 495
JOHN T. FORD ... PROPRIETOR AND MANAGER
(Also of Holliday St. Theatre, Baltimore, and Academy of Music, Phil'a.)
Stage Manager ... J. B. WRIGHT
Treasurer ... H. CLAY FORD

Friday Evening, April 14th, 1865

BENEFIT!
—AND—
LAST NIGHT
OF MISS
LAURA KEENE
THE DISTINGUISHED MANAGERESS, AUTHORESS AND ACTRESS,
Supported by
JOHN DYOTT and HARRY HAWK.

TOM TAYLOR'S CELEBRATED ECCENTRIC COMEDY,
As originally produced in America by Miss Keene, and performed by her upwards of
ONE THOUSAND NIGHTS,
ENTITLED
OUR AMERICAN
COUSIN

FLORENCE TRENCHARD ... MISS LAURA KEENE
(Her original character.)
Abel Murcott, Clerk to Attorney ... John Dyott
Asa Trenchard ... Harry Hawk
Sir Edward Trenchard ... T. C. GOURLAY
Lord Dundreary ... E. A. EMERSON
Mr. Coyle, Attorney ... J. MATTHEWS
Lieutenant Vernon, R. N. ... W. J. FERGUSON
Captain De Boots ... C. BYANES
Binney ... G. G. SPEAR
Buddicomb, a valet ... J. H. EVANS
John Whicker, a gardener ... J. L. De BONAY
Bailiffs ... G. A. PARKHURST and L. JOHNSON
Mary Trenchard ... Miss J. GOURLAY
Mrs. Mountchessington ... Mrs. H. MUZZY
Augusta ... Miss. H. TRUEMAN
Georgina ... Miss M. HART
Sharpe ... Mrs. J. H. EVANS
Skillet ... Miss M. GOURLAY

PATRIOTIC SONG AND CHORUS
"HONOR TO OUR SOLDIERS."
Words by H. B. Phillips; Music Composed and Arranged by Prof. William Withers, Jr.; Solos by Miss M. Hart, H. B. Phillips and George M. Arth, and the Ladies and Gentlemen of the Company.

SATURDAY EVENING, APRIL 15,
BENEFIT of Miss JENNIE GOURLAY
THE OCTOROON
EDWIN ADAMS

NATIONAL PARK SERVICE

Major Henry R. Rathbone

NATIONAL PARK SERVICE

Washington D.C.
April 16th /65

My Dear Mother

It was given out during the day that Mrs. Lincoln had engaged a "box" for the president and Gen. Grant. Before we went Beck knew that the Gen. would not be there as he was to leave for his home in the evening. In the midst of the 2nd scene there was a great applause & cheering and our attention was directed from the stage to the dress circle—close to the wall—walked Miss Harris—Mrs. Lincoln—Major Rathbone—a gentleman the President & another gentleman behind him. We followed him with our eyes until he entered the box little thinking we were looking for the last time at him.

Your aff. dau.
HELEN DuB.

To reach his box, Mr. Lincoln, first entering the theater by its main doorway from Tenth Street, passed through the lobby to the stairs which he climbed to the level of the balcony floor.

W. J. FERGUSON,
call boy at Ford's.

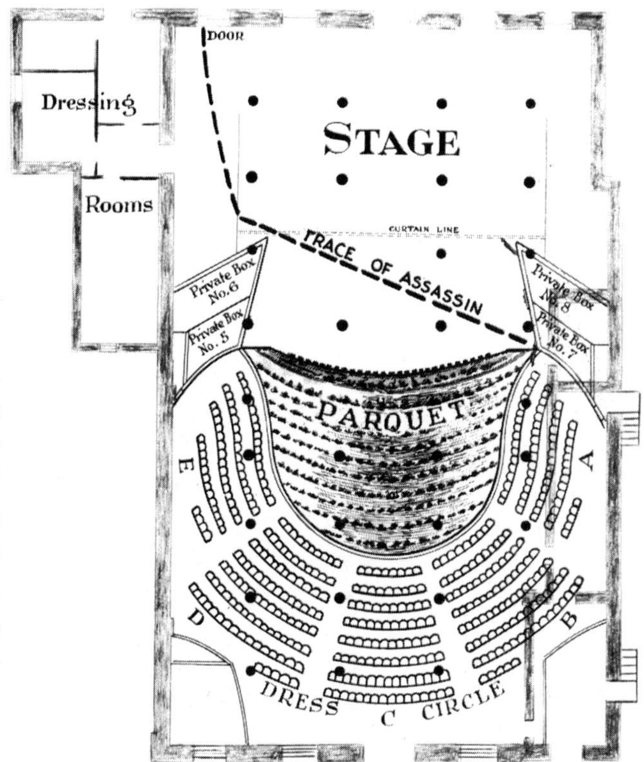

The Dress Circle NATIONAL PARK SERVICE

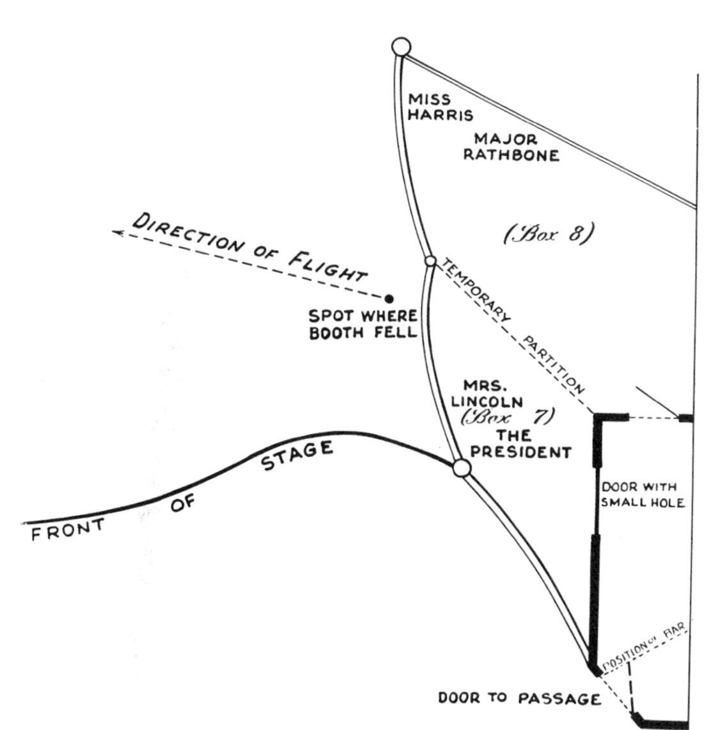

NATIONAL PARK SERVICE

The box assigned to the President is in the second tier on the right-hand side of the audience entered (through) a small entry or passageway, about eight feet in length and four feet in width. This passageway is entered by a door which opens on the inner side. The door is so placed as to make an acute angle between it and the wall behind it on the inner side. At the inner end of this passageway is another door, standing squarely across, and opening into the box. On the left-hand side of the passageway, and being near the inner end, is a third door, which also opens into the box. This latter door was closed.

The party entered the box through the door at the end of the passageway. The box is so constructed that it may be divided into two by a movable partition, one of the doors described opening into each. The front of the box is about ten or twelve feet in length, and in the center of the railing is a small pillar overhung with a curtain. The depth of the box from front to rear is about nine feet. The elevation of the box above the stage, including the railing, is about ten or twelve feet.

Mrs. Lincoln was seated in a chair between the President and the pillar in the centre. At the opposite end of the box, that nearest the stage, were two chairs, in one of these, standing in the corner, Miss Harris was seated. At her left hand, and along the wall running from that end of the box to the rear, stood a small sofa. At the end of this sofa, next to Miss Harris, this deponent was seated. The distance between this deponent and the President, as they were sitting, was about seven or eight feet, and the distance between this deponent and the door was about the same. The distance between the President, as he sat, and the door was about four or five feet.

MAJOR HENRY R. RATHBONE.

NATIONAL PARK SERVICE

When the party entered the box, a cushioned arm chair was standing at the end of the box furthest from the stage and nearest the audience. The President seated himself in this chair and, except that he once left the chair for the purpose of putting on his overcoat, remained so seated until he was shot.

MAJOR RATHBONE.

It was the custom for the guard who accompanied the President to the theater to remain in the little passageway outside the box. Mr. Buckingham remembers that a chair was placed there for the guard on the evening of the 14th. Whether Parker occupied it at all I do not know. If he did, he left it almost immediately; for he confessed to me the next day that he went to a seat in the front of the first gallery, so that he could see the play. The door of the President's box was shut; probably Mr. Lincoln never knew that the guard had left his post. And to think that in that one moment of test one of us should have utterly failed in his duty. He looked like a convicted criminal the next day.

WILLIAM H. CROOK,
one of Lincoln's personal guards.

NATIONAL PARK SERVICE

ILLINOIS STATE HISTORICAL LIBRARY

Lieutenant Crawford and I went to the right side, and took seats in the passage above the seats of the dress circle, and about five feet from the door of the box occupied by President Lincoln. During the performance the attendant of the President came out and took the chair nearest the door. I sat, and had been sitting, about four feet to his left and rear for some time.

Some time after I was disturbed in my seat by the approach of a man who desired to pass up on the aisle in which I was sitting. Giving him room by bending my chair forward, he passed me, and stepped one step down on the level below me. Standing there, he was almost in my line of sight, and I saw him, while watching the play.

He stood, as I remember, one step above the messenger, and remained perhaps one minute apparently looking at the stage and orchestra below. Then he drew a number of visiting cards from his pocket, from which, with some attention, he drew or selected one. I saw him stoop, and I think, descend to the level of the messenger, and as my attention was then more closely fixed upon the play, I do not know whether the card was carried in by the messenger, or his consent given to the entrance of the man who presented it.

I saw, a few minutes after, the same man entering the door of the lobby leading to the box and closing the door behind him. How long after entering I do not know. It was perhaps, two or three minutes, possibly four. The house was perfectly still, the large audience listening to the dialogue. CAPTAIN THEODORE McGOWAN,

Assistant Adjutant General.

"Hopeton" near Washington
April 16, 1865

Dear Father: The President is in yonder upper right hand private box so handsomely decked with silken flags festooned over with a picture of Washington. The young and lovely daughter of Senator Harris is the only one of the party we can see, as the flags hide the rest. How sociable it seems, like one family sitting around their parlor fire.

Everyone has been so jubilant for days, since the surrender of Lee, that they laugh and shout at every clownish witticism. One of the actresses, whose part is that of a very delicate young lady, talks of wishing to avoid the draft, when her lover tells her "not to be alarmed for there is no more draft," at which the applause is long and loud. The American cousin has just been making love to a young lady, who says she will never marry but for love, yet when her mother and herself find he has lost his property they retreat in disgust at the left of the stage. We are waiting for the next scene. . . .

JULIA ADELAIDE SHEPARD.

MUSEUM OF THE CITY OF NEW YORK

John Wilkes Booth

The Assassin of the President is about five nine and a half inches high, black hair, and I think eyes of the same color. He did not turn his face more than quarter front, as artists term it. His face was smooth, as I remember, with the exception of a moustache of moderate size, but of this I am not positive. He was dressed in a black coat, approximating to a dress frock, dark pants, and wore a stiff-rimmed, flat topped round crowned black hat of felt, I think. He was a gentlemanly looking person, having no decided or obtruding mark. He seemed for a moment or two to survey the house with the deliberation of an habitué of the theatre.

CAPTAIN McGOWAN.

BERGHAUS SKETCH, FRANK LESLIE'S ILLUSTRATED NEWSPAPER, APRIL 29, 1865

When the second scene of the third act was being performed, and this deponent was intently observing the proceedings upon the stage, with his back towards the door, he heard the discharge of a pistol behind him, and looking around, saw through the smoke a man between the door and the President. At the same time deponent heard him shout some word which deponent thinks was "Freedom!" This deponent instantly sprang towards him and seized him. He wrested himself from the grasp and made a violent thrust at the breast of deponent with a large knife. Deponent parried the blow by striking it up, and received a wound several inches deep in his left arm between the elbow and the shoulder. The man rushed to the front of the box and deponent endeavored to seize him again, but only caught his clothes as he was leaping over the railing of the box. As he went over upon the stage deponent cried out with a loud voice, "Stop that man!" MAJOR RATHBONE.

The Spur

NATIONAL PARK SERVICE

A moment afterward a hatless and white-faced man leaped from the front of the President's box down twelve feet, to the stage. As he jumped the spurs in his riding boots caught in the folds of the flag.

DR. CHARLES SABIN TAFT,
Assistant Surgeon, U.S. Volunteers.

"In jumping broke my leg." John Wilkes Booth's Diary

BERGHAUS SKETCH, FRANK LESLIE'S ILLUSTRATED NEWSPAPER, MAY 6, 1865.

Clara Harris

LINCOLN NATIONAL LIFE FOUNDATION

Clara H. Harris, being duly sworn, says that at the time she heard the discharge of a pistol she was attentively engaged in observing what was transpiring upon the stage, and looking around she saw Major Rathbone spring from his seat and advance to the opposite side of the box; that she saw him engaged as if in a struggle with another man, but the smoke with which he was enveloped prevented this deponent from seeing distinctly the other man; that the first time she saw him distinctly was when he leaped from the box upon the stage; that she then heard Major Rathbone cry out, "Stop that man," and this deponent then immediately repeated the cry, "Stop that man," "Won't somebody stop that man?" A moment after, some one from the stage asked, "What is it?" or "What is the matter?" and deponent replied, "The President is shot."

Deponent (Major Rathbone) then turned to the President. His position was not changed. His head was slightly bent forward and his eyes were closed. Deponent saw that he was unconscious, and, supposing him mortally wounded, rushed to the door for the purpose of calling medical aid. On reaching the outer door of the passageway deponent found it barred by a heavy piece of plank, one end of which was secured in the wall and the other rested against the door. It had been so securely fastened that it required considerable force to remove it. This wedge or bar was about four feet from the floor. Persons upon the outside were beating against the door. Deponent removed the bar and the door was opened.

BERGHAUS SKETCH, FRANK LESLIE'S ILLUSTRATED NEWSPAPER, MAY 20, 1865

As the person jumped over and lit on the stage, I saw it was Booth. As he struck, he rose and exclaimed, "Sic semper tyrannis!" and ran directly across the stage to the opposite door.

JAMES P. FERGUSON,
for the prosecution.

DIAGRAM OF STAGE

A —— Harry Hawk
B —— Miss Laura Keene
C —— W. J. Ferguson
F —— William Withers, Jr.

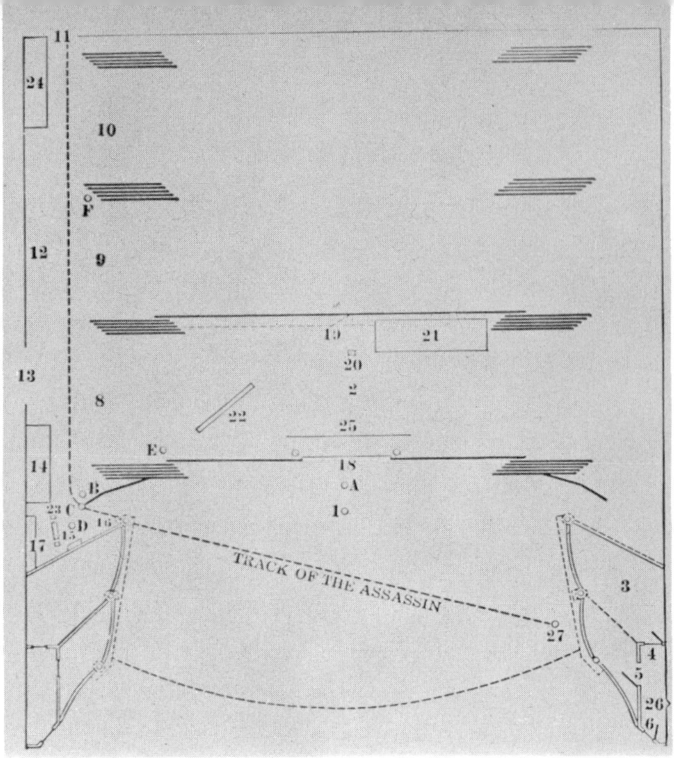

FROM BENN PITMAN

I heard the shot fired, I turned, saw him jump from the box, and drop to the stage; he slipped when he gained the stage, but he got up on his feet in a moment, brandished a large knife, saying "The South shall be free!" turned his face in the direction I stood, and I recognized him as John Wilkes Booth. He ran towards me, and I, seeing the knife, thought I was the one he was after, ran off the stage and up a flight of stairs.

HARRY HAWK,
comedian and Miss Keene's stage manager.

He rushed across the stage toward the first entrance where Miss Keene and I were standing and ran between, so close that I felt his breath on my face. Without pausing he ran to the angle of the north wall and followed it back thirty feet to the little door.

W. J. FERGUSON,
call boy at Ford's.

I am the leader of the orchestra at Ford's Theater. I was returning to the orchestra, when I heard the report of a pistol. I heard some confusion, and saw a man running toward me with his head down. As he ran I could not get out of his way, so he hit me on the leg, and turned me round, and made two cuts at me, one on the neck and one on the side, and knocked me from the third entrance to the second. As I turned I saw it was John Wilkes Booth. He then made a rush for the back door, and out he went.

WILLIAM WITHERS, JR.,
for the prosecution.

Then followed cries that the President had been murdered. I instantly arose, and in response to cries for help and a surgeon I crossed the aisle and vaulted over the seats in a direct line to the President's box forcing my way through the excited crowd. The door of the box had been securely fastened on the inside. The obstruction was removed with difficulty and I was the first to be admitted to the box. Major Rathbone had bravely fought the assassin. His arm had been severely wounded and was bleeding. Mrs. Lincoln and Miss Harris were standing by the high-backed armchair in which President Lincoln sat. I grasped Mrs. Lincoln's outstretched hand in mine while she cried piteously to me: "Oh Doctor, is he dead? Can he recover? Will you take charge of him? Do what you can for him. Oh, my dear husband!" etc.

While approaching the President, I asked a gentleman to procure some brandy and another to get some water. As I looked at the President, he appeared to be dead. His eyes were closed and his head had fallen forward. He was being held upright in the chair by Mrs. Lincoln, who was weeping bitterly. From his crouched-down sitting posture it was evident Mrs. Lincoln had instantly sprung to his aid after he had been wounded and had kept him from tumbling to the floor.

I placed my finger on the President's right radial pulse, but could perceive no movement of the artery. For the purpose of reviving him, if possible, we removed him from his chair to a recumbent position on the floor box, and as I held his head and shoulders while doing this, my hand came in contact with a clot of blood near his left shoulder. Remembering the flashing dagger in the hand of the assassin, and the severely bleeding wound of Major Rathbone, I supposed the President had been stabbed, and while kneeling on the floor over his head, with my eyes continuously watching the President's face, I asked a gentleman to cut the coat and shirt open from neck to elbow. This was done but no wound was found there.

I lifted his eyelids and saw evidence of a brain injury. I quickly passed the separated fingers of both hands through his blood-matted hair to examine his head, and then I discovered his mortal wound. The President had been shot in the back part of the head, behind the left ear. I easily removed the obstructing clot of blood from the wound and this relieved the pressure on the brain. The history of surgery fails to record a recovery from such a fearful wound and I have never seen or heard of any other person with such a wound and injury to the sinus of the brain and to the brain itself who lived even for an hour.

DR. CHARLES A. LEALE,
Assistant Surgeon, U.S. Volunteers.

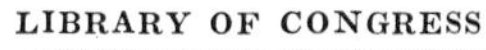
LIBRARY OF CONGRESS

Dr. Charles A. Leale

I leaped from the top of the orchestra railing in front of me upon the stage, and, announcing myself as an Army surgeon, was immediately lifted up to the President's box by several gentlemen who had collected beneath. When I entered the box the President was lying on the floor, surrounded by his wailing wife and several gentlemen who had entered from the private stairway and dress circle. Assistant Surgeon Charles A. Leale was in the box, and had caused the coat and waistcoat to be cut off in searching for the wound.

DR. TAFT.

The crowd behind us surged forward, and our party found itself wedged against the orchestra. My mother, fearing for my safety, undertook to lift me up on the stage; but the pressure from behind became so great that she was unable to extricate me. I might have been injured but for the effort of a somewhat muscular man who picked me up and literally threw me over upon the stage. I could not see the President, but I could hear the loud and turbulent cries of people all over the house. I grew deathly sick and my face must have betrayed me, for the actor who personated Lord Dundreary, E. A. Emerson, noticing me, took off his wig and fanned me vigorously.

People were rapidly clambering upon and filling the stage, when some well-intentioned person, seeing me in the surging mass and anxious to put me out of harm's way, lifted me into the box immediately beneath the one in which the stricken President lay. But so many persons had crowded into the box above that it was feared the floor might give way under the great weight, and I was soon removed. The actors and actresses and other women on the stage huddled together in little groups, quivering with excitement and fear. The whole scene, with its confusion, its grief and tears and terror, was indescribable.

MISS PORTERFIELD.

NATIONAL PARK SERVICE

This knife might have made a wound similar to the one I received. The assassin held the blade in a horizontal position and it came down with a sweeping blow from above.

MAJOR RATHBONE.

The Treasury Flag

NATIONAL PARK SERVICE

As the President did not then revive, I thought of the other mode of death, apnoea, and assumed my preferred position to revive by artificial respiration. I knelt on the floor over the President, with a knee on each side of his pelvis and facing him. I leaned forward, opened his mouth, and introduced two fingers of my right hand as far back as possible, and by pressing the base of his paralyzed tongue downward and outward, opened his larynx and made a free passage for air to enter his lungs. I placed an assistant at each of his arms to manipulate them in order to expand his thorax, then slowly to press the arms down by the side of the body, while I pressed the diaphragm upward; methods which caused air to be drawn in and forced out of his lungs. During the intermissions I also, with the strong thumb and fingers of my right hand, by intermittent sliding pressure under and beneath the ribs, stimulated the apex of heart, and resorted to several other physiological methods.

We repeated these motions a number of times before signs of recovery from profound shock were attained; then followed a feeble action of the heart and irregular breathing followed. I leaned forcibly forward directly over his body, thorax to thorax, face to face, and several times drew in a long breath, then forcibly breathed directly into his mouth and nostrils, which expanded his lungs and improved his respiration. After waiting a moment I placed my ear over his thorax and found the action of the heart improving. I arose to the erect kneeling posture, then watched for a short time and saw that the President could continue independent breathing and that instant death would not occur. I then pronounced my diagnosis and prognosis: "His wound is mortal; it is impossible for him to recover."

While I was kneeling over the President on the floor, Dr. Charles Taft and Dr. Albert F. A. King had come and offered to render any assistance. I expressed the desire to have the President taken, as soon as he gained sufficient strength, to the nearest house on the opposite side of the street. While we were waiting for Mr. Lincoln to gain strength, Laura Keene, who had been taking part in the play, appealed to me to allow her to hold the President's head. I granted this request and she sat on the floor of the box and held his head in her lap. DR. LEALE.

LIBRARY OF CONGRESS

Laura Keene

I had never witnessed such a scene as was now presented. The seats, aisles, galleries, and stage were filled with shouting, frenzied men and women, many running aimlessly over one another; a chaos of disorder beyond control.

I was told that Laura Keene had gone to the assistance of Mrs. Lincoln. I met her at the foot of the staircase leading from the box, and alone. I begged her to tell me if Mr. Lincoln was still alive. "God only knows!" she gasped. The memory of that apparition will never leave me. Attired, as I had so often seen her, in the costume of her part in *Our American Cousin,* her hair and dress were in disorder. But lately the central figure in the scene of comedy, she now appeared the incarnation of tragedy.

SEATON MONROE.

We decided that the President could now be moved from the possibility of danger in the theatre, to a house where we might place him on a bed in safety. To assist in this duty I assigned Dr. Taft to carry his right shoulder, Dr. King to carry his left shoulder, and detailed a sufficient number of others to assist in carrying the body, while I carried his head going first. We reached the door of the box and saw the long passage leading to the exit crowded with people. I called out twice: "Guards clear the passage!"

DR. LEALE.

I went to the box with several others; the bar was lying on the floor inside the first door; I took it up and took it home with me. There was an officer where I was boarding who wanted a piece of the bar and it was sawed off.

ISAAC JAQUETTE,
for the prosecution.

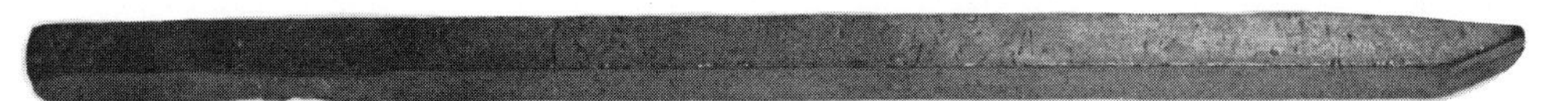

NATIONAL PARK SERVICE

The Bar

About three minutes after the President was shot, I went into his box. A surgeon asked me for a knife to cut open the President's clothing. On leaving the theater I missed my night-key, and thinking I had dropped it in pulling out my knife, I hurried back and searching round the floor of the box, I knocked my foot against a pistol, which I picked up, and, holding it up, I cried out, "I have found the pistol." I gave it to Mr. Gobright, the agent for the Associated Press.

WILLIAM T. KENT,
for the prosecution.

NATIONAL PARK SERVICE

William H. Seward,
Secretary of State

LIBRARY OF CONGRESS

That was the ninth day since the serious carriage accident to Secretary of State Seward and that statesman lay helpless and suffering. The family took turns in watching at his bedside, and two invalid nurses were sent to assist in his care. Night came, and about ten o'clock the gas lights were turned low and all was quiet. In the sick room with the secretary were his daughter Fanny and the invalid soldier nurse, Robinson.

There seemed nothing unusual when a tall, well-dressed, man presented himself below, and, informing the servant that he brought a message from the doctor, was allowed to come up the stairs to the door of Seward's room. He was met here by the assistant secretary, who refused him admission, explaining that the sleeping invalid must not be disturbed. He paused, apparently irresolute. When advised to leave his

The Seward Residence

NATIONAL PARK SERVICE

message and go back to report to the doctor, he replied, "Very well, sir, I will go," and, turning away, took two or three steps down the stairs. Suddenly, turning again, he sprang up and forward, having drawn a navy revolver, which he leveled, with a muttered oath, and pulled the trigger.

And now, in swift succession, like the scenes of some hideous dream, came the bloody incidents of the night—of the pistol missing fire; of the struggle in the dimly lighted hall between the armed man and the unarmed one; of the blows which broke the pistol of the one and fractured the skull of the other; of the bursting in of the door; of the mad rush of the assassin to the bedside, and his savage slashing with a bowie knife at the face and throat of the helpless secretary, instantly reddening the white bandages with streams of blood; of the screams of the daughter for help; of the attempt of the invalid soldier nurse to drag the assailant from his victim, receiving sharp wounds himself in return; of the noise made by the awakening household, inspiring the assassin with hasty impulse to escape, leaving his work done or undone; of his frantic rush down the stairs, cutting and slashing all whom he found in his way, wounding one in the face and stabbing another in the back; of his escape through the open doorway, and his flight on horseback down the avenue.

Five minutes later the aroused household were gazing, horrified, at the bleeding faces and figures in their midst, were lifting the insensible form of the secretary from a pool of blood, and sending for surgical help. Meanwhile, a panic-stricken crowd was surging in from the street, to the hall and rooms below, vainly inquiring or wildly conjecturing what had happened. FREDERICK W. SEWARD.

FROM J. R. HAWLEY'S THE ASSASSINATION

The Attempted Assassination

CHAPTER II

O POWERFUL, WESTERN, FALLEN STAR!

A PRESIDENT DIES

NATIONAL ARCHIVES AND DANIEL W. JONES, NBC

NATIONAL PARK SERVICE

"Borne by Loving Hands," from the painting by Carl Bersch

I had changed my clothes and shut off the gas when we heard such a terrible scream that we ran to the front window to see what it could mean. We saw a great commotion in the theater—some running in, others running out—and we could hear hundreds of voices mingling in the greatest confusion. Presently we heard someone say, "The President is shot!" I hurried on my clothes and ran out across the street as they brought him out of the theater. Poor man!

GEORGE FRANCIS,
a tenant in the Petersen house.

The crowd in the street completely obstructed the doorway, and a Captain came to me saying, "Surgeon, give me your commands and I will see that they are obeyed." I asked him to clear a passage to the nearest house opposite. With sword and a word of command he cleared the way. It was necessary to stop several times to give me opportunity to remove the clot of blood from the wound. Those who went ahead reported the house directly opposite was closed. I saw a man standing at the door of Mr. Petersen's house holding a lighted candle and beckoning us to enter. The great difficulty of retaining life during this brief time conclusively proved that the President would have died in the street, if I had granted the request to take him such a long distance as to the White House.

DR. CHARLES A. LEALE,
Assistant Surgeon, U.S. Volunteers.

They carried him out into the street and into our house, and passed to the little room in the back. Mrs. Lincoln came in soon after. She was perfectly frantic. "Where is my husband? Where is my husband?" she cried, wringing her hands in the greatest anguish. Our front parlor was given up to Mrs. Lincoln and her friends. The back parlor was occupied by Secretary Stanton. Judge Carter held an informal court there and it was full of people.

GEORGE FRANCIS.

He was lifted to the longitudinal centre of the bed and placed on his back. While holding his face upward and keeping his head from rolling to either side, I looked at his elevated knees caused by his great height. This uncomfortable position grieved me, and I ordered the foot of the bed to be removed. Dr. Taft and Doctor King reported that it was a fixture. Then I requested that it be broken off; as I found this could not be satisfactorily done, I had the President placed diagonally on the bed and called for extra pillows and formed a gentle inclined plane on which to rest his head and shoulders.

DR. LEALE.

The wound was then examined. A tablespoon of diluted brandy was placed between the President's lips but it was swallowed with much difficulty. The respiration now became labored; pulse 44, feeble; the left pupil much contracted, the right widely dilated; total insensibility to light in both. Mr. Lincoln was divested of all clothing, and mustard plasters were placed on every inch of the anterior surface of the body from neck to the toes. The eyes were closed, and the lids and surrounding parts so injected with blood as to present the appearance of having been bruised. He was totally unconscious, and was breathing regularly but heavily, an occasional sigh escaping with the breath.

DR. CHARLES S. TAFT,
Assistant Surgeon, U.S. Volunteers.

The wound which I had received had been bleeding very profusely, and on reaching the house, feeling very faint from the loss of blood, I seated myself in the hall, and soon fainted away, and was laid upon the floor. Upon the return of consciousness I was taken to my residence.

MAJOR HENRY R. RATHBONE.

We found the streets crowded with excited masses of people. The first person I met in the hall was Miss Harris. She informed me the President was dying but desired me not to communicate the fact to Mrs. Lincoln. I then entered the front parlor, where I found Mrs. Lincoln in a state of indescribable agitation. She repeated over and over again, "Why didn't he kill me? Why didn't he kill me?" MAUNSELL B. FIELD,
Assistant Secretary of the Treasury.

The room is in the rear part of the building, and at the end of the main hall, from which rises a stairway. The walls are covered with a brownish paper, figured with a white design. Its dimensions are about ten by fifteen feet. Some engravings were copies of the "Village Blacksmith," and Herring's "Stable and Barnyard Scenes." The photograph was one taken from an engraved copy of Rosa Bonheur's "Horse Fair." The only furniture in the room was a bureau covered with crochet, a table, eight or nine plain chairs, and a bed upon which Mr. Lincoln lay when his spirit took its flight. The bedstead was a low walnut, with a headboard from two to three feet high. The floor was carpeted with Brussels, considerably worn. Everything on the bed was stained with the blood of the Chief Magistrate of the nation. ALBERT BERGHAUS,
Illustrator for Frank Leslie's Illustrated Newspaper.

I was the family physician of the Late President. I was sent for by Mrs. Lincoln immediately after the assassination. I arrived in a very few moments. I found among others, two assistant surgeons of the army, who had brought him over from the theater, and who had attended him. They immediately gave the case over to my care. I proceeded to examine the President, and I at once informed those around that the case was a hopeless one. I remained with him, doing whatever was in my power, assisted by my friends; but, of course, nothing could be done. DR. ROBERT KING STONE.

I had not gone far toward the White House before I met a number of men who told me he was not there. I then ran down the Avenue to F Street, down F to Tenth Street, and thence to the theatre, around which I pushed my way and presently I was at the bedside of the dying President. All night we stood or sat silent by his bedside.
HUGH McCULLOCH,
Secretary of the Treasury.

The entire city tonight presents a scene of wild excitement accompanied by violent expressions of indignation and the profoundest sorrow. Many shed tears. The military authorities have dispatched mounted patrols in every direction, in order, if possible, to arrest the assassins. L. A. GOBRIGHT,
Chief, Washington Associated Press.

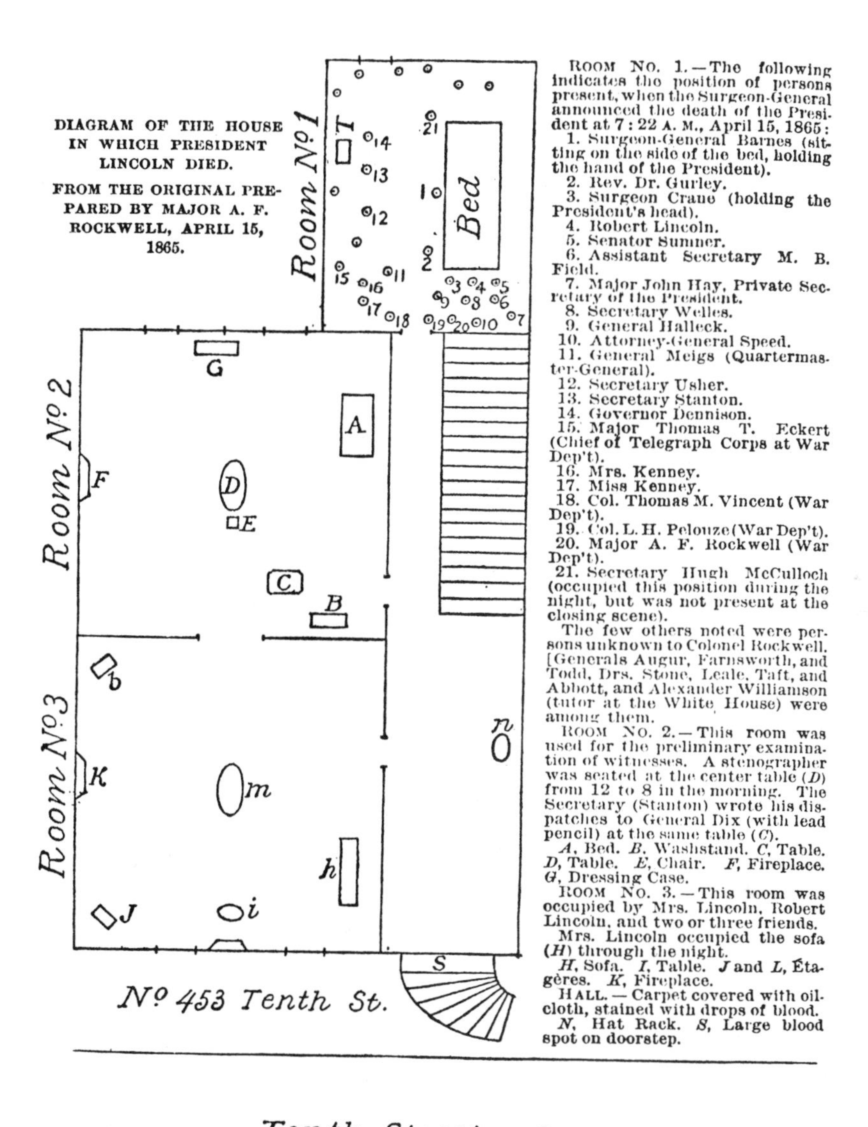

DIAGRAM OF THE HOUSE IN WHICH PRESIDENT LINCOLN DIED.

FROM THE ORIGINAL PREPARED BY MAJOR A. F. ROCKWELL, APRIL 15, 1865.

ROOM NO. 1.—The following indicates the position of persons present, when the Surgeon-General announced the death of the President at 7 : 22 A. M., April 15, 1865:

1. Surgeon-General Barnes (sitting on the side of the bed, holding the hand of the President).
2. Rev. Dr. Gurley.
3. Surgeon Crane (holding the President's head).
4. Robert Lincoln.
5. Senator Sumner.
6. Assistant Secretary M. B. Field.
7. Major John Hay, Private Secretary of the President.
8. Secretary Welles.
9. General Halleck.
10. Attorney-General Speed.
11. General Meigs (Quartermaster-General).
12. Secretary Usher.
13. Secretary Stanton.
14. Governor Dennison.
15. Major Thomas T. Eckert (Chief of Telegraph Corps at War Dep't).
16. Mrs. Kenney.
17. Miss Kenney.
18. Col. Thomas M. Vincent (War Dep't).
19. Col. L. H. Pelouze (War Dep't).
20. Major A. F. Rockwell (War Dep't).
21. Secretary Hugh McCulloch (occupied this position during the night, but was not present at the closing scene).

The few others noted were persons unknown to Colonel Rockwell. [Generals Augur, Farnsworth, and Todd, Drs. Stone, Leale, Taft, and Abbott, and Alexander Williamson (tutor at the White House) were among them.

ROOM NO. 2.—This room was used for the preliminary examination of witnesses. A stenographer was seated at the center table (*D*) from 12 to 8 in the morning. The Secretary (Stanton) wrote his dispatches to General Dix (with lead pencil) at the same table (*C*).

A, Bed. *B*, Washstand. *C*, Table. *D*, Table. *E*, Chair. *F*, Fireplace. *G*, Dressing Case.

ROOM NO. 3.—This room was occupied by Mrs. Lincoln, Robert Lincoln, and two or three friends.

Mrs. Lincoln occupied the sofa (*H*) through the night.

H, Sofa. *I*, Table. *J* and *L*, Étagères. *K*, Fireplace.

HALL.—Carpet covered with oilcloth, stained with drops of blood.

N, Hat Rack. *S*, Large blood spot on doorstep.

FROM NICOLAY AND HAY, VOL. X

Dr. Charles S. Taft

LLOYD OSTENDORF

I was awakened from a sound sleep with the news that Mr. Lincoln had been shot, and that the Secretary wanted me. All the members of the cabinet were gathered in an adjoining parlor. They seemed to be almost as much paralyzed as the unconscious sufferer within the little chamber.

Mr. Stanton alone was in full activity. "Sit down here," he said; "I want you." Then he began and dictated orders one after another, which I wrote out and sent swiftly to the telegraph. All these orders were designed to keep the government in full motion till the crisis should be over. It was perhaps two o'clock in the morning before he said, "That's enough. Now you can go home." CHARLES A. DANA,
Assistant Secretary of War.

(Stanton said he) sent for Johnson, thinking that he ought to be present, but when Mrs. Lincoln wished to come in Mr. Sumner, thinking that she ought not to see Johnson there, and knowing she had a strong personal dislike for him, suggested that he ought to go. So, I told him there was no necessity for his remaining any longer, and he went. EDWIN M. STANTON,
Secretary of War.

About twenty-five minutes after the President was laid on the bed, Surgeon-General Barnes and Dr. Robert King Stone, the family physician, arrived and took charge of the case. It was owing to Dr. Leale's quick judgment in instantly placing the almost moribund President in a recumbent position the moment he saw him in the box, that Mr. Lincoln did not expire in the theater within ten minutes from fatal syncope.
DR. TAFT.

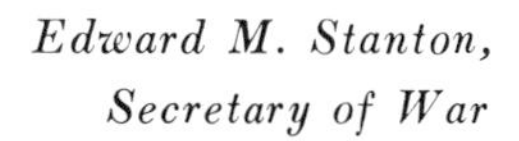

Edward M. Stanton,
Secretary of War

LIBRARY OF CONGRESS

Gideon Welles,
Secretary of the Navy

NATIONAL PARK SERVICE

The giant sufferer lay extended diagonally across the bed, which was not long enough for him. He had been stripped of his clothes. His large arms were of a size which one would scarce have expected from his spare form. His features were calm and striking. I had never seen them appear to a better advantage, than for the first hour I was there. The room was small and overcrowded. The surgeons and members of the Cabinet were as many as should have been in the room, but there were many more, and the hall and other rooms in front were full. GIDEON WELLES,
Secretary of the Navy.

No drug or medicine in any form was administered, but the artificial heat and mustard plaster warmed his cold body and stimulated his nerves. The hospital steward arrived with the Nelaton probe and an examination was made by the Surgeon-General and myself, who introduced the probe to a distance of about two and a half inches, where it came in contact with a foreign substance, which lay across the track of the ball. This was easily passed and the probe was introduced several inches farther, where it again touched a hard substance at first supposed to be the ball; but as the white porcelain bulb of the probe, on its withdrawal, did not indicate the mark of lead, it was generally thought to be another piece of loose bone.

The probe was introduced the second time and the ball was supposed to be distinctly felt. After this nothing further was done except to keep the opening free from coagula, which if allowed to form and remain for a short time produced signs of increased compression, the breathing becoming profoundly stertorous and intermittent, the pulse more feeble and irregular. DR. LEALE.

The streets were filled, and then I heard that the Secretary of State, and his two sons, and nurse had been attacked, and nearly murdered. It was then reported that Gen. Grant had been killed in Philadelphia, and in a short time, they had everybody of any consequence in the city assassinated. It was a night of horror such as I never hope to witness again. JOHN DEERING, JR.,
Clerk in the Treasury.

Robert Lincoln

ILLINOIS STATE HISTORICAL LIBRARY

I went to the house on Tenth street. They would not let me in. The little room was crowded with men who had been associated with the President during the war. They were gathered around the bed watching, while, long after the great spirit was quenched, life little by little loosened its hold on the long, gaunt body. Among them, I knew, were men who had contended with him during his life or who had laughed at him. Charles Sumner stood at the very head of the bed. I know that it was to him that Robert Lincoln, who was only a boy for all his shoulder straps, turned in the long strain of watching. But the room was full and they would not let me in.

William H. Crook,
special guard for the President.

During the night Mrs. Lincoln came frequently from the adjoining room, accompanied by a lady friend. At one time Mrs. Lincoln exclaimed sobbing bitterly, "Oh! that my little Taddy might see his father before he died!" As Mrs. Lincoln sat on a chair by the side of the bed with her face to her husband's, his breathing became very stertorous and the loud unnatural noise frightened her. She sprang up suddenly with a piercing cry and fell fainting to the floor. Secretary Stanton, hearing her cry, came in from the adjoining room and with raised arms called out loudly, "Take that woman out and do not let her in again." Dr. Leale.

The night was dark, cloudy, and damp, and about six it began to rain. I remained in the room without sitting or leaving it—there being a vacant chair which someone left at the foot of the bed, I occupied it for nearly two hours, listening to the heavy groans, and witnessing the wasting life of the good and great man who was expiring before me.

About six A.M. I experienced a feeling of faintness, and for the first time after entering the room, a little past eleven, I left it and the house, and took a short walk in the open air. It was a dark and gloomy morning, and the rain set in before I returned to the house, some fifteen minutes (later).

Large groups of people were gathered every few rods, all anxious and solicitous. Some one or more from each group stepped forward as I passed, to enquire into the condition of the President, and asked if there was no hope. Intense grief was on every countenance.

Returning to the house, I seated myself in the back parlor where the Attorney-General and others had been engaged in taking evidence. Stanton, and Speed, and Usher were there—the latter asleep in the bed. A little before seven I went into the room where the dying President was rapidly drawing near the closing moments. His wife soon after made her last visit to him. The death struggle had begun.

GIDEON WELLES.

The respiration during the last thirty minutes was characterized by occasional intermissions; no respiration being made for nearly a minute, but by a convulsive effort air would gain admission to the lungs, when regular though stertorous respiration would go on for some seconds, followed by another period of perfect repose.

The vitality exhibited by Mr. Lincoln was remarkable. It was the opinion of the surgeons that most patients would have died within two hours from the reception of such an injury; yet Mr. Lincoln lingered from 10:30 P.M. until 7:22 A.M. Outside a drizzling rain was falling upon the heads of a multitude that were packed from Pennsylvania Avenue as far as the eye could see. DR. TAFT.

At last the physician said: "He is gone; he is dead." Then I solemnly believe that for four or five minutes there was not the slightest noise or movement in that awful presence. We all stood transfixed in our positions, speechless, around the dead body of that great and good man. The Secretary of War, who was standing at my left, said: "Doctor, will you say anything?" I replied, "I will speak to God." When I had ceased, there arose from the lips of the entire company a fervid and spontaneous "Amen."

DR. PHINEAS D. GURLEY,
the Lincoln family's pastor.

A look of unspeakable peace came over his worn features. Stanton broke the silence by saying, "Now he belongs to the ages."

JOHN HAY,
the President's personal secretary.

On the following page
"Final Hours," from the painting by Alexander H. Ritchie LIBRARY OF CONGRESS

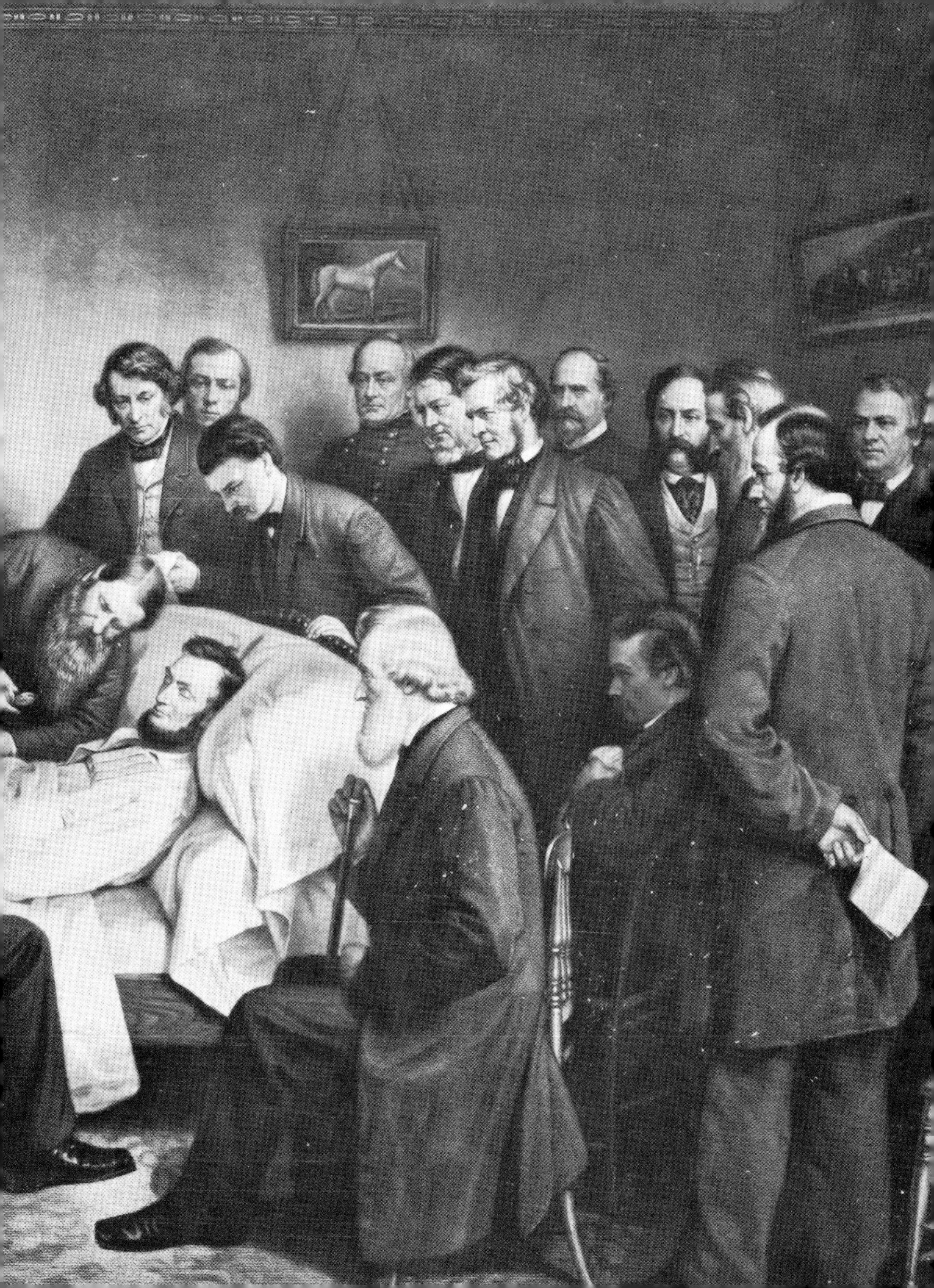

A prayer followed from Dr. Gurley; and the Cabinet, with the exception of Mr. Seward and Mr. McCulloch, assembled in the back parlor and there signed a letter to the Vice-President informing him the government devolved upon him.

GIDEON WELLES,
Secretary of the Navy.

I joined Mr. Petersen's son—a lad with whom I chummed; and went with him through the basement of the house to the stairs in the rear. Climbing them, we came to the floor of the room where Mr. Lincoln had been taken. It was a room formerly occupied by a Mr. Mathews, still a member of our company. I had delivered parts during the season to him and others in the room. On one of these visits I saw John Wilkes Booth lying and smoking a pipe on the same bed in which Mr. Lincoln died.

W. J. FERGUSON.

Shortly after his death I entered the front parlor, and found Mrs. Lincoln supported in the arms of her son. As she reached the front door, she glanced at the theater opposite, and exclaimed several times, "Oh, that dreadful house! That dreadful house!"

MAUNSELL B. FIELD.

I stepped to the window and saw the coffin of the dead President being placed in the hearse which passed up Tenth street to F and thus to the White House. As they passed with measured tread and arms reversed, my hand involuntarily went to my head in salute as they started on their long, long journey back to the prairies and the hearts he knew and loved so well, the mortal remains of the greatest American of all time.

CORPORAL JAMES TANNER.

We rode at full speed to the White House, but all was quiet there, a policeman hailed us and told us that the President had been shot at Ford's theater. We hastened to the place and found that the street was blocked with a great crowd. We were ordered to clear the street for one block in front of the house where the President lay. Having cleared the street, we remained there on guard the balance of the night.

It was an awful night. To be awakened out of a sound sleep and to be brought face to face with a tragedy so shocking made it hard for me to realize that it could be true. All night I rode slowly up and down the street in front of that house. Sometimes I would pinch myself and wonder if I was really awake, so hard was it for me to realize the fact that President Lincoln was lying in that house in a dying condition.

SERGEANT SMITH STIMMEL,
of the President's Mounted Guard.

FRANK LESLIE'S ILLUSTRATED NEWSPAPER, MAY 20, 1865

Early Morning at the Petersen House

NATIONAL ARCHIVES

Joseph K. Barnes, Surgeon-General

Surgeon-General Barnes, assisted by Doctors Stone, Curtis, Woodward, Crane, Taft, and other eminent medical men, made an autopsy. The external appearance of the face of the President presented a deep black stain around both eyes. The fatal wound was on the left side of the head, behind, in a line with and three inches from the left ear. The course of the ball was obliquely forward toward the right eye, crossing the brain in oblique manner, and lodging a few inches behind that eye.

In the track of the wound were found fragments of bone which had been driven forward by the ball, which were imbedded in the anterior lobe of the left hemisphere of the brain. The orbit plates of both eyes were the seat of comminuted fracture and the eyes were filled with extravasated blood. The wound was about one-half inch in diameter.

It was a large ball, resembling those which are shot from the pistol known as the Derringer; an unusually large ball. It was a leaden handmade ball, and was flattened somewhat in its passage through the skull. This is the ball which I extracted from the head of the President.

DR. STONE.

The Ball

NATIONAL PARK SERVICE

Washington, D.C., April 19, 1865

Dear Sister Ida:

Hundreds daily call at the house to gain admission to my room, I was engaged nearly all day Sunday with one of Frank Leslie's special artists, aiding him in making a complete drawing of the last moments of Mr. Lincoln. He succeeded in executing a fine sketch, which will appear in their paper.

Everybody has a great desire to obtain some memento from my room, so that whoever comes in has to be closely watched for fear they will steal something. I have a lock of Mr. Lincoln's hair, which I have had neatly framed; also a piece of linen with a portion of his brain.

The pillow and case upon which he lay when he died, and nearly all his wearing apparel, I intend to send to Robert Lincoln as soon as the funeral is over. The same mattress is on my bed, and the same coverlid covers me nightly that covered him while dying.

I will write again soon.

Your affec. brother,

WILLIE.

NATIONAL PARK SERVICE

William T. Clark

CHAPTER III

I MOURN'D AND YET

LIBRARY OF CONGRESS

A WASHINGTON FUNERAL

SHALL MOURN

When we had sufficiently collected ourselves to dress and go out of doors in the bleak and cheerless April morning, we found in the streets an extraordinary spectacle. They were suddenly crowded with people—men, women and children thronging the thoroughfares. It seemed as if everyone was in tears. Pale faces streaming eyes, with now and again an angry, frowning countenance were on every side.

But at half-past seven o'clock in the morning the tolling of the bells announced to the lamenting people that he had ceased to breathe. His great and loving heart was still. Instantly flags were raised at half-mast all over the city, the bells tolled solemnly, and with incredible swiftness Washington went into deep, universal mourning. All stores, government departments, and private offices were closed, and everywhere, on the most pretentious residences, and on the humblest hovels, were the black badges of grief.

Nature seemed to sympathize in the general lamentation, and tears of rain fell from a moist and somber sky. The wind sighed mournfully through the streets crowded with sad-faced people, and broad folds of funeral drapery flapped heavily in the wind over the decorations of the day before.

Wandering aimlessly up F street toward Ford's Theatre, we met a tragical procession. It was headed by a group of army officers walking bareheaded, and behind them was the bier of the dead President, covered with the flag of the Union, and accompanied by an escort of soldiers. As the little cortege passed down the street to the White House, every head was uncovered, and profound silence which prevailed was broken only by sobs and by the sound of the measured tread of those who bore the martyred President back to the home which he had so lately quitted full of life, hope, and courage.

NOAH BROOKS.

ILLINOIS STATE HISTORICAL LIBRARY

Among journalists, Lincoln's most intimate confidant was Noah Brooks (Castine) of the Sacramento Union, *who accompanied the President on battlefield tours, was a frequent White House visitor and family friend. Lincoln planned to have Brooks succeed Nicolay as private secretary.*

NATIONAL PARK SERVICE

Mary Lincoln

At nine o'clock we took her home to that house so changed for her—& the Dr said she must go immediately to bed. She refused to go into any of the rooms she had previously occupied, "not there! oh not there" she said—& so we took her to one she had arranged for the President for a summer room to write in—I remained till eleven o'clock (twelve hours from the time I went to her) and then left her a lonely widow, everything changed for her, since they left so happily the evening previous. As I started to go down stairs I met the cortege bringing up the remains of the murdered President.

Your sister very affectionately

E. I. Dixon.

Tad Lincoln

ILLINOIS STATE HISTORICAL LIBRARY

Saturday April 15, 1865. A dismal day. After breakfast I went to the White House. Soon after the body of the President was brought in, he having died at 7:20 this morning. Robert Lincoln told me his mother did not wish to go back to Springfield and did not want his father's remains taken there, but to Chicago, if any where in Illinois. I did not see Mrs. Lincoln—she was greatly agitated and in bed.

ORVILLE BROWNING,
former Senator from Illinois.

When Mr. Lincoln's body had been removed to the President's House, the embalmers proceeded to prepare it for the grave. Mr. Harry P. Cattell, in the employ of Doctors Brown and Alexander, who, three years before, had prepared so beautifully the body of little Willie Lincoln, now made as perpetual as art could effect the peculiar features of the late beloved President. The body was drained of its blood, and the parts necessary to remove to prevent decay were carefully withdrawn, and a chemical preparation injected, which soon hardened to a consistence of stone, giving the body the firmness and solid immobility of a statue.

At the White House all was silent and sad. Mrs. W. was with Mrs. L. and came to meet me in the library, (Attorney General) Speed came in, and we soon left together. As we were descending the stairs, "Tad," who was looking from the window at the foot, turned and, seeing us, cried aloud in his tears, "Oh, Mr. Welles, who killed my father?" Neither Speed nor myself could restrain our tears, nor give the poor boy any satisfactory answer.

GIDEON WELLES.

My Dear Wife,

Today has been the saddest day of my life, if indeed one day can be sadder than another of the sad days that has shrouded the nation in gloom. I have no words to express what I feel and how much I now long to fold you to my bosom and mingle my burning tears with yours for the loss of our greatest, best & most kind and loving friend, Abraham Lincoln. Now that he has gone to the Spirit land we realize how much we loved him and how worthy he was of our love and confidence.

After recovering my composure, I sought the presence of poor heart broken Mrs. Lincoln. I found her in bed more composed than I had anticipated, but the moment I came within her reach she threw her arms around my neck and wept most hysterically for several minutes, and this completely unmanned me again, but my sympathy was to her most consoling, and for a half hour she talked most composedly about what had transpired between her and her Husband that day and evening of his death, which I will tell you when we meet.

She says he was more cheerful and joyous that day and evening than he had been for years. When at dinner he complained of being worn out with the incessant toils of the day, and proposed to go to the Theatre and have a laugh over the Country Cousin. She says she discouraged going, on account of a bad headache, but he insisted that he must go, for if he stayed at home he would have no rest for he would be obliged to see company all the evening as usual.

Finding that he had decided to go, she could not think of having him go without her, never having felt so unwilling to be away from him. She sat close to him and was leaning on his lap looking up in his face when the fatal shot was fired, his last words being in answer to her question "What will Miss Harris think of my hanging on to you so"—"She won't think anything about it"—and said accompanied with one of his kind and affectionate smiles. . . .

ANSON.

ILLINOIS STATE HISTORICAL LIBRARY

One of the President's very few close friends was Dr. Anson G. Henry. This strong personal bond had its beginnings with Lincoln's enigmatic collapse following the broken engagement with Mary Todd in 1841. In 1861 the President had named his friend as Surveyor General of Washington Territory and during his frequent trips to the Capitol, the doctor was often in Lincoln's company, sometimes as a guest in the White House.

Homes near Ford's Theatre ILLINOIS STATE HISTORICAL LIBRARY

The Capitol NATIONAL PARK SERVICE

John Hay

In 1860 Lincoln engaged as private secretary twenty-eight-year-old newspaperman and devoted admirer, John G. Nicolay. Before departing for the Capitol, Nicolay induced the President-elect to employ as an assistant John M. Hay, a twenty-three-year-old Springfield law student. No one was more intimately associated with the Lincoln administration than these two extraordinary young White House roommates. ILLINOIS STATE HISTORICAL LIBRARY

John G. Nicolay

The appalling news spread quickly over the country; millions of citizens learned at their breakfast tables that the President had been shot and was dying; and after his death when a squad of soldiers were escorting his mortal remains to the Executive Mansion, the dreadful fact was known to all the great centers of population.

This was the first time the telegraph had been called upon to spread over the world tidings of such deep and mournful significance; it was therefore the first time the entire people of the United States had been called to deplore the passing away of an idolized leader even before his body was cold in death. The news fell with peculiar severity upon hearts which were glowing with the joy of a great victory.

For the last four days, in every city and hamlet of the land, the people were breaking forth into unusual and fantastic expressions of gaiety and content; bonfires flamed through the nights; the days were uproarious with the firing of guns; the streets were hung with flags and wreaths and committees were everywhere forming to arrange for elaborate and official functions of joy.

Upon this mirth and expansion the awful intelligence from Washington fell with the crushing and stunning effect of an unspeakable calamity. In the sudden rigor of this unexpected misfortune the country lost sight of the vast national success of the past week; and it thus came to pass that there was never any organized expression of the general exultation or rejoicing in the North over the downfall of the rebellion.

It was unquestionably best that it should be so; and Lincoln himself would not have had it otherwise. He hated the arrogance of triumph; and even in his cruel death he would have been glad to know that his passage to eternity would prevent too loud an exultation over the vanquished. JOHN G. NICOLAY AND JOHN HAY.

Ford's Theatre NATIONAL PARK SERVICE

When on the morning of April 15th, the news that the President had been murdered was communicated to the people, the nation's joy was turned to mourning. Flags which had been hung out as tokens of rejoicing were draped in mourning and public meetings—spontaneous gatherings of the people—expressive of unfeigned regret and intense indignation, were held.

Bloomington, Illinois, April 18, 1865

TREMENDOUS EXCITEMENT

The Popular Heart Affected

Immense Meeting on Sunday

A SABBATH WELL SPENT

6,000 PEOPLE PRESENT

The different pastors of the city were turned out to speak. Nearly every one of them spoke eloquent words of comfort, of patriotism, of loyalty and cheering assurance of God's certainty to bring light out of the darkness. On behalf of the people we desire to thank our ministers for the noble and sensible and practical stand they took on this great occasion.

CHICAGO HISTORICAL SOCIETY

Photograph by J. W. Tankerly of scene at Court House Square, Bloomington, Illinois, April (16), 1865, representing mass meeting expressing grief and profound indignation over assassination of Abraham Lincoln. (*Photographer's notation*)

She was nearly exhausted with grief, and when she became a little quiet, I received permission to go into the Guest Room, where the body of the President lay in state. When I crossed the threshold of the room I could not help recalling the day on which I had seen little Willie lying in his coffin where the body of his father now lay. I remembered how the President had wept over the pale beautiful face of his gifted boy, and now the President himself was dead. ELIZABETH KECKLEY,

Mrs. Lincoln's dressmaker, maid and confidante.

Monday April 17, 1865. Then went to the Executive Mansion and again saw the corpse of the President which was greatly changed since Saturday, and was looking as natural as life, and if in a quiet sleep. We all think the body should be taken to Springfield for interment, but Mrs. Lincoln is vehemently opposed to it, and wishes it to go to Chicago. ORVILLE BROWNING.

On the night of the 17th the remains were taken to the famous East Room, and there they lay in state until the day of the funeral (April 19). The great room was draped with crape and black cloth, relieved only here and there by white flowers and green leaves. The catafalque upon which the casket lay was fifteen feet high, and consisted of an elevated platform resting on a dais and covered with a domed canopy of black cloth which was supported by four pillars and was lined beneath with fluted white silk.

From the time the body had been made ready for burial until the last services in the house, it was watched night and day by a guard of honor. At the head and foot and on each side of the casket of their dead chief stood the motionless figures of his armed warriors. NOAH BROOKS.

On the 18th of April arrangements were completed. The doors would not be opened until 10 o'clock that morning, and by 9:30 the line, four and six persons deep, was nearly a quarter of a mile long. The arrangements at the house for entrance and exit were: entrance at the main door, thence to the Green Room, thence to the East Room, and out at the window by the customary steps. It was estimated that 25,000 persons passed through the rooms, and that half as many more, seeing the immense throng, left without trying to get in. Two to three hours was the average period of waiting, and many waited even five and six hours.

After the body was laid "in state" at the White House, I with my friends stood in line from 10 A.M. until 2 P.M. that we might see his face once more. The crowd was so great that one moved with the throng without an effort of his own, our escorts standing "akimbo" to keep off the crush. At the entrance to the grounds, we were met by soldiers who stood with fixed bayonets under which only a few were allowed to pass at a time. At the door other soldiers, with their muskets crossed, allowed half the number in the house, once in, around the catafalque, and out at another door before others were let in; but in that brief moment I gazed into the face that had shone with such happiness as he said he could see his way clearly. "Surely everything is clear to him now," I thought.

The coffin was six feet six inches in length, and one foot and a half across the shoulders. It was of mahogany, and lined with lead, covered with superb black broadcloth, and with four massive handles upon each side. There was a heavy bullion fringe extending entirely around the edge of the upper part. The large silverplate was in the centre of a shield formed with silver tacks, on which was the inscription

ABRAHAM LINCOLN
SIXTEENTH PRESIDENT OF THE UNITED STATES
Born February 12, 1809
Died April 15, 1865

NATIONAL PARK SERVICE

The Coffin

LIBRARY OF CONGRESS *The Washington Hearse*

The hearse was a splendid piece of mechanism. The lower base was fourteen feet long and seven feet wide, and eight feet from the ground. The upper base, on which the coffin rested was eleven feet long, and was five feet below the top of the canopy. The canopy was surmounted by a gilt eagle covered with crape. The whole hearse was covered with cloth, velvet, crape and alpaca. The seat was covered with hammer-cloth, and on each side was a splendid black lamp. The hearse was fifteen feet high, and the coffin so placed as to afford a full view to all spectators. It was drawn by six gray horses.

The troops designated to form the escort will assemble in the Avenue north of the President's house, and form a line precisely at 11 o'clock A.M., on Wednesday, the 19th instant, with the left resting on Fifteenth street. The procession will move precisely at 2 o'clock P.M., on the conclusion of the religious services at the Executive Mansion (appointed to commence at 12 o'clock M.), when minute guns will be fired by detachments of artillery stationed near St. John's Church, the City Hall, and at the Capitol. At the same hour the bells of the several churches in Washington, Georgetown, and Alexandria will be tolled. At sunrise on Wednesday, the 19th instant, a Federal salute will be fired from the military stations in the vicinity of Washington, minute guns between the hours of 12 and 3 o'clock, and a national salute at the setting of the sun. By order of the Secretary of War. W. A. NICHOLS,

Assistant Adjutant General.

LIBRARY OF CONGRESS

The most noteworthy report of the events of this day was telegraphed to the New York World by its gifted 24-year-old war-correspondent, George Alfred Townsend (Gath).

Washington, April 19 (Evening)

Deeply ensconced in the white stuffing of his coffin, the President lies like one asleep. The lid is drawn back to show the face and bosom. This coffin set upon a platform and canopied, has around it a sufficient space of Brussels carpet, and on three sides of this are raised steps covered with black, on which the honored visitors are to stand. All is rich, simple, and spacious. Approach and look at the dead man.

Death has fastened into his frozen face all the character and idiosyncrasy of life. He has not changed one line of his grave, grotesque countenance, nor smoothed out a single feature. The hue is rather bloodless and leaden; but he was always sallow. The dark eyebrows seem abruptly arched; the beard, which will grow no more, is shaved close, save the tuft at the short small chin. The mouth is shut, like that of one who had put the foot down firm, and so are the eyes, which look as calm as slumber.

The collar is short and awkward, turned over the stiff elastic cravat, and whatever energy or humor or tender gravity marked the living face is hardened into its pulseless outline. No corpse in the world is better prepared according to appearances. All that we see of Abraham Lincoln, so cunningly contemplated in this splendid coffin, is a mere shell, an effigy, a sculpture. He lies in sleep, but it is the sleep of marble. All that made this flesh vital, sentient, and affectionate is gone forever.

The funeral guns are heard indistinctly booming from the far forts, with the tap of drums in the serried street without, where troops and citizens are forming for the grand procession. We see through the window in the beautiful spring day that the grass is brightly green; and all the trees in blossom.

But there is one at an upper window, seeing all this through her tears. The father of her children, the confidant of her affection and ambition, has passed from life into immortality, and lies below, dumb, cold, murdered. The feeling of sympathy for Mrs. Lincoln is as widespread as the regret for the chief magistrate.

ILLINOIS STATE HISTORICAL LIBRARY

Admission Ticket

SOUTH.

Admit the Bearer to the
EXECUTIVE MANSION,
On WEDNESDAY, the
19th of April, 1865.

Whatever indiscretions she may have committed in the abrupt transition from plainness to power are now forgiven, and forgotten. She and her sons are the property of the nation, associated with its truest glories and its worst bereavement.

By and by the guests drop in, hat in hand, wearing upon their sleeves waving crape. With these are sprinkled many scarred and worthy soldiers who have borne the burden of the grand war. Closer to the catafalque rest the familiar faces of our greatest generals but sitting on a chair upon the beflowered carpet is Ulysses Grant who comes today to add luster of his iron face to this thrilling and saddened picture. He is swarthy, nervous and almost tearful. What think the foreign ambassadors of such men! These legations number perhaps a hundred men.

But nearer down stand the central powers of our government, its President and counsellors. President Johnson is facing the middle of the coffin, beside him is Vice-President Hamlin, whom he succeeded. The cabinet are behind as if arranged for a daguerreotypist, Stanton, short and quicksilvery, in long goatee and glasses, in stunted contrast to the tall and snow-tipped shape of Mr. Welles.

This scene is historic. I regret that I must tell you of it over a little wire. The religious services began at noon. They were remarkable not only for the tremendous political energy which they had.

Reverend Dr. Hall opened the service by reading from the Episcopal service for the dead. This was followed by an eloquent and affecting prayer by Bishop Simpson of the Methodist Church. At the close of his fervent appeal to the throne of Grace the Bishop repeated the Lord's Prayer, in which the whole audience joined as with one voice. Rev. Dr. Gurley, the pastor of the church which the President and his family were in the habit of attending, preached the funeral discourse. The service was closed with prayer by Rev. Dr. Gray, chaplain of the Senate.

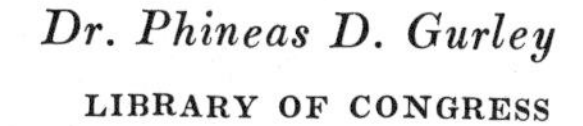

Dr. Phineas D. Gurley
LIBRARY OF CONGRESS

Services at the White House (on the following page)
FRANK LESLIE'S ILLUSTRATED NEWSPAPER, MAY 6, 1865

The Cortege Moving Past the President's Mansion

Not less than five thousand officers, of every rank, marched abreast with the cortege. They were noble-looking men with intelligent faces, and represented the sinews of the land, and the music was not the least excellent feature of the mournful display. About thirty bands were in the line, and these played all varieties of solemn marches, so that there was continual and mingling strain of funeral music for more than three hours. Artillery, consisting of heavy brass pieces, followed behind. Never again, until Washington becomes in fact, what it is in name, the chief city of America, shall we

FRANK LESLIE'S ILLUSTRATED NEWSPAPER, MAY 6, 1865

have a scene like this repeated—the grandest procession ever seen on this continent, spontaneously evoked to celebrate the foulest crime on record. If any feeling of gratulation could arise in so calamitous a time, it would be, that so soon after this appalling calamity the nation calmly and collectedly rallied about its succeeding rulers, and showed in the same moment its regret for the past and its resolution for the future. To me, the scene in the White House, the street, and the Capitol today, was the strongest evidence the war afforded of the stability of our institutions, and the worthiness and magnanimous power of our people.

The procession surpassed in sentiment, populousness, and sincere good feeling, anything of the kind we have had in America. It was several miles long, and in all its elements was full and tasteful. The scene on the avenue will always be remembered as the only occasion on which that great thoroughfare was a real adornment to the seat of government. In the tree tops, on the house tops, at all the windows, the silent and affected crowds clustered beneath half-mast banners and waving crape, to reverentially uncover as the dark vehicle, bearing its rich-silver-mounted coffin, swept along; mottoes of respect and homage were on many edifices. The chief excellence of the procession was its representative nature. All classes, localities and trades were out. As the troops in broad, straight, columns, with reversed muskets, moved to solemn marches, all the guns on the fortifications on the surrounding hills discharged hoarse salutes—guns which the arbiter of war whom they were to honor could hear no longer.

The Procession on Pennsylvania Avenue
HARPER'S WEEKLY, MAY 6, 1865

On the Avenue

ILLUSTRATED LONDON NEWS, MAY 20, 1865

Those who were privileged to entrance to the Capitol were universal in their declarations that it was the grandest and most imposing demonstration they had ever seen. It appeared to us like a grand panorama, in which the figures were statuesque, and gradually presented to view.

Long before the solemnities began at the White House, crowds of people flocked to the Capitol. It was arranged that the funeral procession should pass up the north side of the Capitol, and enter the building at the central door of the east front. Inside there reigned a solemn silence broken only by the thunder of artillery just beyond the Capitol grounds.

The tolling of bells and the minute-guns from the forts announced that the cortege was forming, and made the solemnity of the deserted Capitol almost oppressive. The mournful pageant could be discerned moving slowly down the grand avenue—moving, and yet it did not seem to move, so gradual was its advance.

In the center of the marble floor stood the catafalque, covered with black. Just after three o'clock the head of the cortege wheeled into the open space in front of the eastern entrance. When the infantry extended quite across the open space they halted and faced inward, thus enclosing the entrance in a military square. The artillery passed behind the infantry, and took position on the hill opposite the entrance. The cavalry remained without in the street. The officers of the army and navy gathered in great groups in front of the infantry.

Finally the carriages rolled slowly up to deposit the mourners who formed in double line up the steps leading to the east door. On either hand and behind the soldiers throngs of spectators looked silently on. A sad burst of melodies filled the air, and the funeral car stopped to allow Abraham Lincoln to enter the Capitol for the last time.

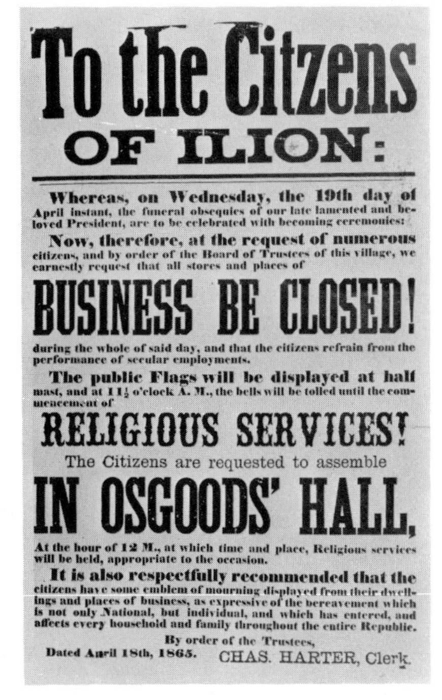

To the Citizens
OF ILION:

Whereas, on Wednesday, the 19th day of April instant, the funeral obsequies of our late lamented and beloved President, are to be celebrated with becoming ceremonies:

Now, therefore, at the request of numerous citizens, and by order of the Board of Trustees of this village, we earnestly request that all stores and places of

BUSINESS BE CLOSED!

during the whole of said day, and that the citizens refrain from the performance of secular employments.

The public Flags will be displayed at half mast, and at 11½ o'clock A. M., the bells will be tolled until the commencement of

RELIGIOUS SERVICES!

The Citizens are requested to assemble

IN OSGOODS' HALL,

At the hour of 12 M., at which time and place, Religious services will be held, appropriate to the occasion.

It is also respectfully recommended that the citizens have some emblem of mourning displayed from their dwellings and places of business, as expressive of the bereavement which is not only National, but individual, and which has entered, and affects every household and family throughout the entire Republic.

By order of the Trustees,

Dated April 18th, 1865. CHAS. HARTER, Clerk.

Observances were held in all the towns and villages

The Second Inauguration LIBRARY OF CONGRESS

Six weeks and a half ago President Lincoln stood upon a platform built over the very same steps up which he was now being carried, and delivered his second inaugural address.

The coffin was posted under the bright concave, now streaked with mournful trappings, and left in state, watched by guards of officers with drawn swords. This was a wonderful spectacle, the man most beloved and honored in the ark of the republic. The storied paintings representing eras in its history were draped in sable, through which they seemed to cast reverential glances upon the lamented bier.

At night the jets of gas concealed in the spring of the dome were lighted up, so that their bright reflection upon the frescoed walls hurled masses of burning light, like marvelous haloes, upon the little box where so much that we love and honor rested on its way to the grave. And so through the starry night, in the fane of the great Union he had strengthened and recovered, the ashes of Abraham Lincoln are now reposing.

As soon as the doors were thrown open on the morning of the 20th, the throng of visitors began. All were required to enter at the main eastern entrance, and, passing in two lines on either side of the catafalque, to go out the western door of the rotunda.

The procession of saddened faces came pressing forward at the rate of three thousand persons per hour. The rotunda, which was lighted only by a sort of twilight hue, was filled with solemn stillness, unbroken save by the rustling of the dresses of the female mourners, and occasionally a deep sigh from some of those passing the coffin. At six o'clock the doors of the Capitol were closed to visitors.

While this solemn pageant was passing, I was allowed to go alone up the winding stairs that led to the top of the great dome of the Capitol. Looking down from that lofty point, the sight was weird and memorable. Directly beneath me lay the casket in which the dead President lay at full length, far, far below; and like black atoms moving over a sheet of gray paper, the slow-moving mourners, seen from a perpendicular above them, crept silently in two dark lines across the pavement of the rotunda, forming an ellipse around the coffin and joining as they advanced toward the western portal and disappeared.

On the morning of Friday, the 21st, I went to the Capitol at 6 A.M. The object being to have but few present when the remains were taken from the rotunda, where they had lain in state through Thursday. I wished also to take my sons with me to the obsequies, the last opportunity they or I would have to see the remains and to manifest our respect and regard for the man who had been the steady and abiding friend of their father.

We reached the Capitol and entered the rotunda just as Mr. Gurley was commencing an earnest and impressive prayer. When it was concluded, the remains were removed and taken to the depot, where, in waiting, were a car and train prepared for the commencement of the long and circuitous journey of the illustrious dead to his last earthly resting place in Springfield, in the great prairies of the West.

GIDEON WELLES.

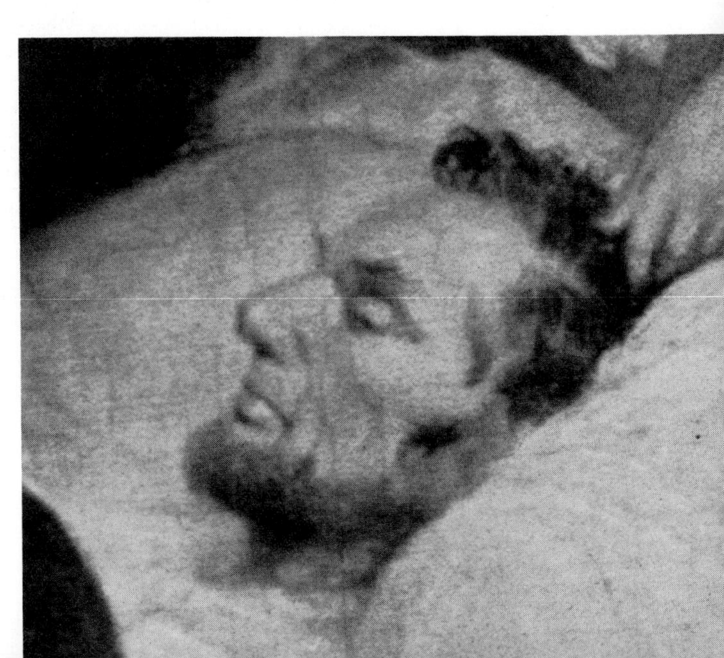

Segment from the painting designed by John B. Bachelder and painted by Alonzo Chappel

MCCLELLAN LINCOLN COLLECTION, BROWN UNIVERSITY

CHAPTER IV

NIGHT AND DAY

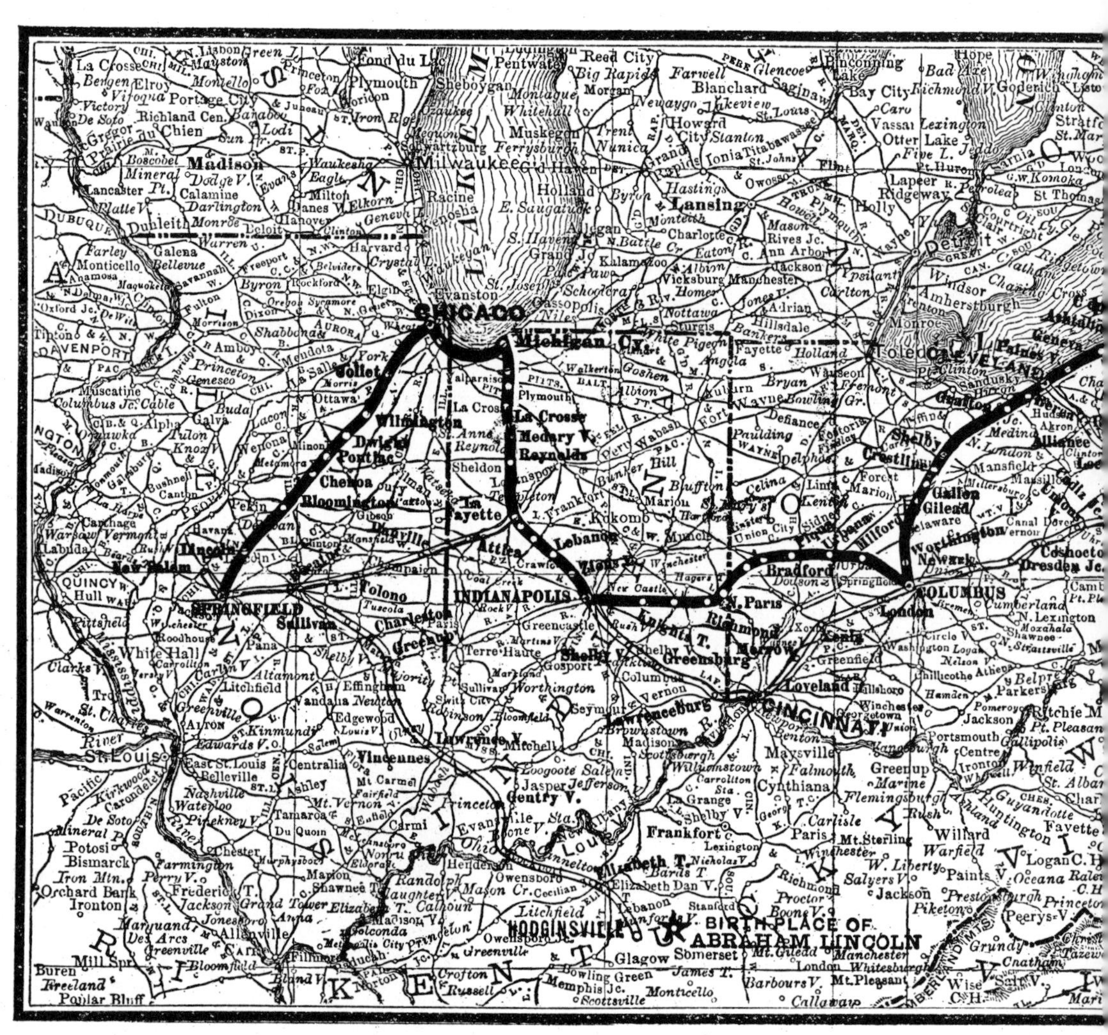

FROM POWER'S THE LIFE OF LINCOLN

JOURNEYS A COFFIN

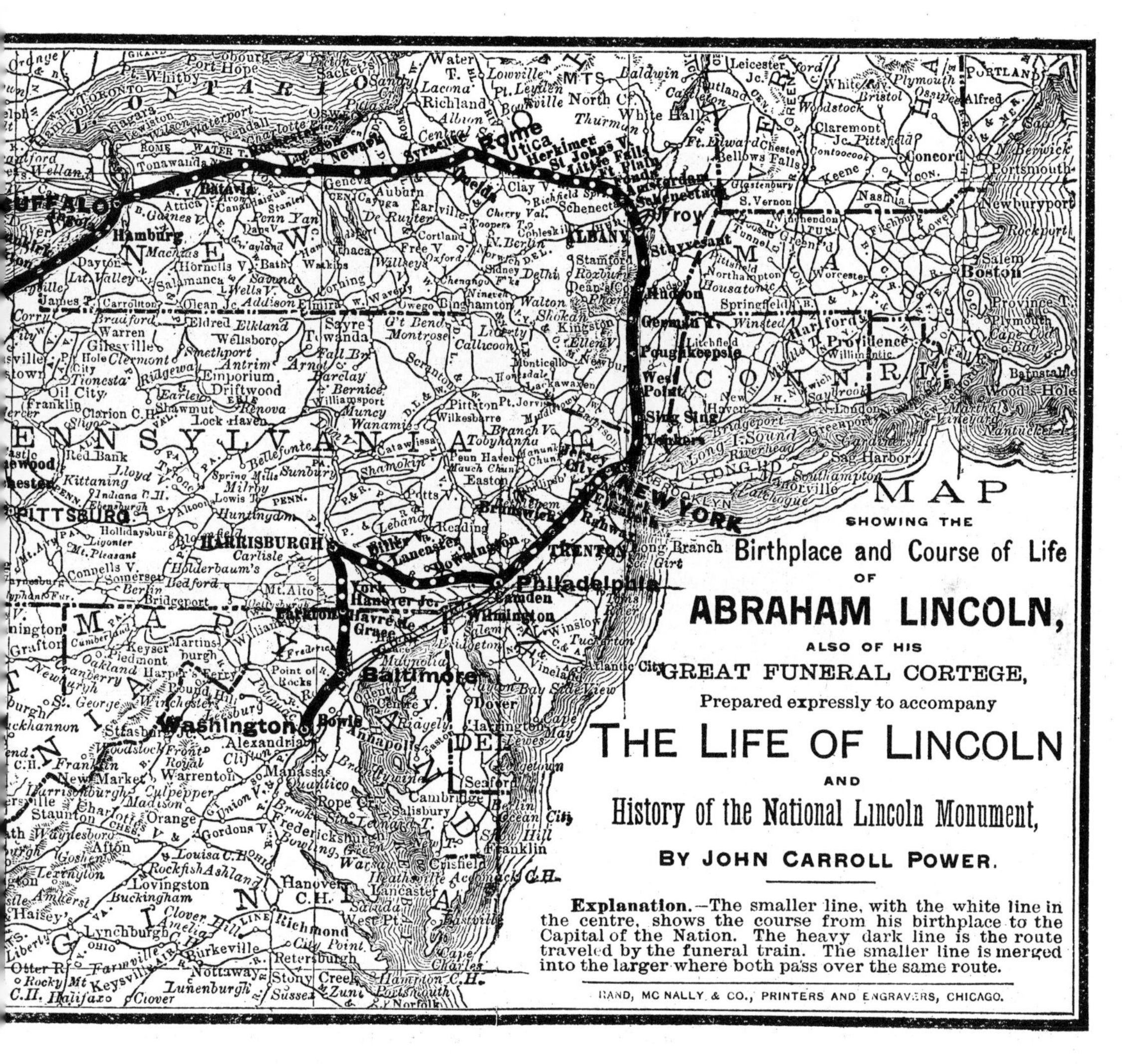

THE MOURNING PAGEANT

The funeral of Abraham Lincoln! How can justice be done to the theme? The obsequies continued through sixteen days and sixteen nights. History has no parallel to the outpouring of sorrow which followed the funeral cortege on its route from Washington to Springfield.

Hundreds of thousands of men, women, and children crowded the highways and streets, by day and by night, to do reverence to those mortal remains. Often would they kneel in silent prayer. Many wept in quiet. The shocking deed by which the President had been taken from his people seemed to intensify their love and veneration for his memory.

MAJOR GENERAL E. D. TOWNSEND,
in charge of the train.

COURTESY ILLINOIS CENTRAL RAILROAD

The Funeral Train at Chicago

The funeral train consisted of nine cars, eight of them furnished in succession by the chief railroads over which the remains were transported. This route differs from that taken by Mr. Lincoln on his way to Washington in 1861 only by omitting Cincinnati and Pittsburg, and by making detour by way of Chicago, instead of going direct from Indianapolis to Springfield.

Twenty-one first sergeants of the Veteran Reserve Corps accompanied the remains as a guard. A few minutes before eight o'clock, Rev. Dr. Gurley, standing upon the platform, made the following impressive prayer: "O Lord our God, strengthen us under the pressure of this great national sorrow. . . ."

The Funeral Car NATIONAL PARK SERVICE

The funeral car is a model of chaste and beautiful workmanship. It is forty-two feet long, with twelve windows on each side. The color of the car is dark claret, beautifully polished. The platforms of the car are of brass and steel, they are highly finished and ornamented. On the outside of the car is painted the coat of arms of the United States.

This moving palace was built at the U.S. Military shops in Alexandria. It cost about $12,000 and was presented to, and intended solely for the use of, the late President. Alas! That it should be his funeral bier. Outside and inside, the car is draped in heavy, sombre colors. Silver fringe hangs from the car, below which is heavy drapery of black, trimmed with silver bullion, and ornamented with silver tassels pendant between the windows.

The remains of little Willie Lincoln, who died in the White House (February 20, 1862) at the age of twelve years, were placed in the interior of the hearse car, immediately in front of those of his father. Mrs. Lincoln requested that no display be made of her son's remains, but that they might be privately removed to Springfield.

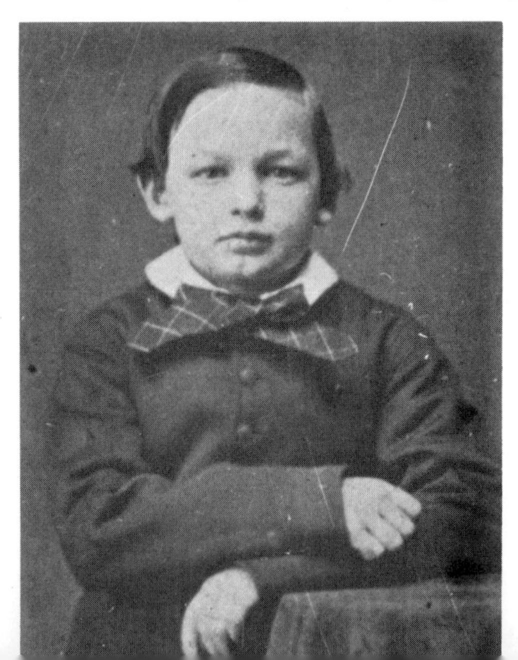

Willie Lincoln
ILLINOIS STATE HISTORICAL LIBRARY

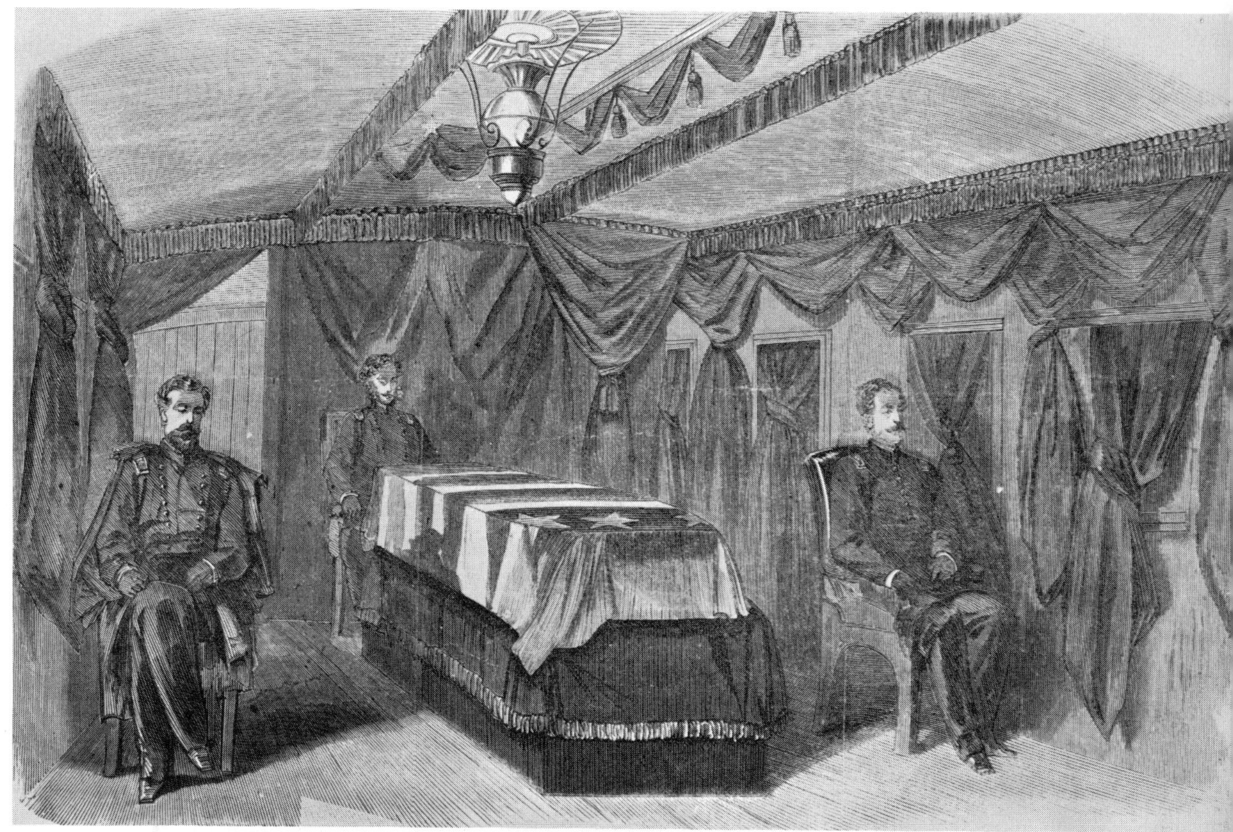

NATIONAL PARK SERVICE

The Interior

The inside is a perfect palace. The sides are upholstered with magenta red. The window curtains are of silk damask festooned and trimmed with green fringe. The floor is covered with a handsome Brussels carpet. The furniture is made of black walnut and covered with green plush. On the small panels round the opening in the top of the car are painted the coat of arms of all the states. The car is divided in three compartments of equal size. The center room is enclosed as a state room and elegantly furnished. The interior of the car presents a sorrowfully beautiful appearance.

Its sides are draped in black, tastefully festooned about the windows and over the doorways, and relieved by small glittering silver stars that shine very brightly. On one side of the state room, lying upon a pedestal draped in black, is the coffin containing the earthly remains of little Willie Lincoln. At the other end of the car repose the remains of Abraham Lincoln. The coffin was placed upon a pedestal which is covered by a magnificent flag draped in black.

THE SCHEDULE

Leave Washington, Friday, April 21, 8 A.M.
Arrive at Baltimore, Friday, April 21, 10 A.M.
Leave Baltimore, Friday, April 21, 3 P.M.
Arrive at Harrisburg, Friday, April 21, 8:20 P.M.
Leave Harrisburg, Saturday, April 22, 12 M.
Arrive at Philadelphia, Saturday, April 22, 4:30 P.M.
Leave Philadelphia, Monday, April 24, 4 A.M.
Arrive at New York, Monday, April 24, 10 A.M.
Leave New York, Tuesday, April 25, 4 P.M.
Arrive at Albany, Tuesday, April 25, 11 P.M.
Leave Albany, Wednesday, April 26, 4 P.M.
Arrive at Buffalo, Thursday, April 27, 7 A.M.
Leave Buffalo, Thursday, April 27, 10:10 P.M.
Arrive at Cleveland, Friday, April 28, 7 A.M.
Leave Cleveland, Friday, April 28, midnight.
Arrive at Columbus, Saturday, April 29, 7:30 A.M.
Leave Columbus, Saturday, April 29, 8 P.M.
Arrive at Indianapolis, Sunday, April 30, 7 A.M.
Leave Indianapolis, Sunday, April 30, midnight.
Arrive at Chicago, Monday, May 1, 11 A.M.
Leave Chicago, Tuesday, May 2, 9:30 P.M.
Arrive at Springfield, Wednesday, May 3, 8 A.M.

The Funeral Coach at Harrisburg

ILLINOIS STATE HISTORICAL LIBRARY

BALTIMORE

Arrive Friday, April 21, 10 A.M.
Leave Friday, April 21, 3 P.M.

Action of the City Council

Mayor's Office City Hall
April 20, 1865

The remains of the late President of the United States will arrive in this city on tomorrow (Friday) morning, on the way to its last resting place in Springfield, Illinois, and as the last token of respect to the deceased, it is desirable that the citizens generally should unite with the State and military authorities on that occasion.

Baltimore, April 21.—The body of President Lincoln arrived here at 10 o'clock, and the procession is now moving. The display is very fine. There is an immense turn out of citizens, and a very large escort of artillery, cavalry, infantry, marines and sailors. The stores are all closed; the whole population is in the streets; bells are tolling, and minute guns are firing; the weather is unpleasant, a mist is falling, and the lowering sky adds to the sadness which is depicted on every countenance.

The buildings are everywhere draped in the emblems of grief. The body is to lie in state until two o'clock in the Rotunda of the Exchange, beneath the splendid dome. The interior of the building is elegantly draped. A splendid catafalque, erected of rich materials, is placed in the centre, and the body rests upon a dais strewn with white flowers.

In the civic procession appears all the clergy of the city on foot. The rear of the procession is made up of a very large turn out of colored persons.

The funeral ceremonies at Baltimore were particularly impressive. Nowhere were the manifestations of grief more universal; but the sorrow of the negroes, who thronged the streets in thousands, and hung like a dark fringe upon the long procession, was especially impressive. Their coarse, homely features were convulsed with a grief which they could not control. Their emotional natures were excited by the scene, and by each other, until sobs and cries, and tears rolling down their black faces, told how deeply they felt their loss. ISAAC N. ARNOLD,
of the Illinois delegation.

HARRISBURG
Arrive Friday, April 21, 8:35 P.M.
Leave Saturday, April 22, 12 M.

Precisely at twenty-five minutes of 9 o'clock the car containing the remains was pulled up the track to the center of Market Street. The arrival was announced by a salute of twenty-one guns and the tolling of the bells of the city.

At about half-past eight a heavy rain storm set in, accompanied with vivid flashes of lightning and rolling peals of thunder. In other times, and under other circumstances, the first phenomenon of the season, indicating the departure of Winter and arrival of Spring, would have been hailed with gladness; but, in addition to bringing with it the greatest discomfort to thousands, it required but little stretch of fancy to imagine it as typical of the national gloom and of heaven's wrath upon the bloody crime that had been committed.

The rain continued almost unceasingly the entire night. On the arrival of the remains of the late President, the rain became so violent it was almost unendurable. The civic portion of the procession sought shelter in door-ways and under awnings but the military bravely stood the pelting shower.

The rain continued throughout the night. The day opened rather warmer, but still cloudy with frequent heavy showers of rain. Thousands of men, women and children thronged at the Capitol grounds to obtain a view of the remains. State Street and all the approaches to the Capitol were swarming with people long before the procession was ready to move. About nine o'clock all the civic delegations marched through the Capitol in double file, and took a last view of the remains of the illustrious dead.

The Train at Harrisburg LINCOLN NATIONAL LIFE FOUNDATION

CHICAGO HISTORICAL SOCIETY

The Completed Preparations

The coffin containing the remains was placed in the center of the Hall of the House of Representatives, on a raised form in front of the Speaker's desk, which was heavily draped and festooned with crape. The head of the coffin was placed toward the Speaker's desk, so that as the procession filed in by twos through the main door they diverged at the foot of the coffin, passed in single file on each side, securing a close but brief glance at the face of the remains. At 12 o'clock the Hall was closed to visitors, and the guard for the night was set.

The hearse was drawn to the Capitol gates. On its approach the bands present struck up a mournful dirge, and the coffin was brought and placed in position, the cortege moved in line, at twenty minutes past ten o'clock to the depot. About eleven o'clock the whistle of the locomotive sounded departure, and the sad cortege moved slowly off. The vast concourse of people composing the procession was then formally dismissed; the military took their ways to camp and barracks, and soon our streets assumed the quietness and desertion of a Sunday in midsummer.

PHILADELPHIA
Arrive Saturday, April 22, 4:30 P.M.
Depart Monday, April 24, 4 A.M.

Philadelphia
April 21, 1865

Dear Brother:

The whole Country from Cairo here is Draped in Mourning. Everything in the Country has stopped perfectly still—Excepting these Yankees here—they are Making fortunes out of it—by selling Badges of Mourning with Mr. Lincolns Photograph—also Cards with dates of Birth and Account of his birthplace—besides his "life and Public Services"

3 o'clock P.M. 22 inst. The remains of our beloved President have just arrived in the city and the Minute Guns are thundering forth his Glory. The procession is to pass down the street upon which I am stopping and the Crowd is beginning to gather along the street now by the thousands and tis some *three* Hours yet until the Procession is to begin to pass. I will stop writing until after the Ceremonies are over when perhaps I can give you some idea of it. . . . HENRY S. WILSON.

The train reached the Baltimore depot at Broad and Washington. Hours before, tens of thousands of men, women, and children had crowded all the streets leading to this great avenue. The procession was formed and moved to Independence Hall, the grounds being illuminated with calcium lights, red, white and blue colors, with a splendid band performing funeral dirges. The coffin was taken into Independence Hall and placed on a platform directly opposite "Old Independence Bell."

And thus Abraham Lincoln, the martyr of the nineteenth century, was laid in solemn repose beneath the roof which once covered the grand old heroes and statesmen of the Revolution. On the 22nd of February he was in that Hall, and under the inspiration of its sacred memories, while raising the national flag above its hallowed roof, he uttered these significant words:

> ". . . But if this country cannot be saved without giving up that principle, I was about to say, I would rather be assassinated upon this spot than to surrender it. . . ."

The hearse, especially constructed for the occasion, was an imposing structure, well adapted for its purpose, which was to display the coffin to view as prominently as possible. It was drawn by eight black horses, with silver mounted harness.

At fifteen minutes past five the hearse, followed by the special guard of honor, on foot, and the carriages commenced to move, the military taking its place in advance, keeping time to the slow, solemn music of the bands and the melancholy tolling of the bells. The funeral procession through the streets numbered one hundred thousand, and three hundred thousand more were spectators.

ILLINOIS STATE HISTORICAL LIBRARY

Six o'clock, Sabbath morning was fixed as the hour when the remains were to be exhibited to public view. Long before the hour arrived, thousands of people were on the streets and formed into lines. The entrances were through two windows on Chestnut street, and the exits through the windows facing them on Independence Square, temporary steps having been placed in position.

So great was the anxiety to view the body that hundreds remained all night. At the hour of six o'clock double lines of applicants were formed, extending as far west as Eighth street, and east to Third. By eleven o'clock the lines extended from the Hall west as far as the Schuylkill, and east as far as the Delaware. So it was throughout the day and night, until one o'clock on the morning of the 24th, and thousands found themselves disappointed.

Many women lost their bonnets, while others had nearly every particle of clothing torn from their persons. After a person was once in line, it took from four to five hours before an entrance to the Hall could be effected.

Sunday 23d 4 P.M. Dear Brother: I told you last P.M. that I would wait until the Honors had been paid to the Illustrious dead—when I might give you some idea of it—the Ceremonies are not over yet—and tis impossible for you to form any idea of its immensity—the processions of Men, Women, Children & Negroes is from three to five Miles long on all the different streets leading to the Hall—and they are not in double file—but as thick as it is possible for them to crowd on the side walks. There are only two Entreances by which the visitors can get in the Hall to see the Remains—and the jam to get in beats any thing I ever saw or Heard of in my life. O Brother you can not imagine what a Sight I have seen this day—that you may have some idea of the density of the people you can imagine an immense building with forty or fifty thousand people Men Women and children all crowding and striveing to get in at two small enterences. There has been over a Hundred Women Fainted in the Midst of the Jam, and strange as it may seem—yet tis true, I saw three little boys who had been smothered that were lifted up from the ground and placed upon the Heads of the People until they revived, when they succeeded in crauling upon the heads of the

LINCOLN NATIONAL LIFE FOUNDATION

FROM TRIAL OF THE ALLEGED ASSASSINS

Mass until they finally got out back from the building whare the Crowd was not so dense and got out barely with there lives—Now since I have told you how nearly impossible it is for any one to get into the hall to see the remains without being Jamed almost, if not to death, you will wonder how I a Stranger got in without being mashed. 'Twas in this way. I called around to the Continental—(by the way the finest Hotel I ever saw) this A.M. to look over the Register and had been there but a few Moments when I meet Govenor Oglesby, Senator Yates and several other distinguished Illinoisans.

The Govnr. recognized me—and after a little talk he invited me accompany him and them to visit "Independance Hall." . . . our Admittance was disputed by the police for a while but we finally were permitted to Enter . . . I saw the pale face of Mr. Lincoln several times before we left—from that room we were conducted into the Council Chambers up stairs and twas from the Windows up there that we saw this sea of Human beings Struggling and Mashing Each other to death to get in to see the remains of the President. . . . Even now this late 5 P.M. the people are still striving by the thousands to get in to see the Illustrious dead.

The Number of People including Visitors in the City now—are Estimated at Nine Hundred and Fifty Thousand (950,000) Just think of Even one fourth of that number endeavoring to crowd through two ordinary door ways in one day. I have undoubtedly saw the—largest Mass of Human Beings—and the Grandest Sight to day that I shall ever see again. Would to Heaven that you and Harry could have been with me. . . .

HENRY S. WILSON.

Funeral Car Crossing Hudson River FROM VALENTINE

NEW YORK
Arrive Monday, April 24, 11 A.M.
Leave Tuesday, April 25, 4:15 P.M.

In the streets of Jersey City every housetop, every balcony, every window overlooking the road taken by the procession, from the depot to the ferry, was crowded with spectators. Slowly the corpse was borne, amidst the solemn booming of minute-guns and the tolling of distant bells, to the ferry-boat "Jersey City."

All the shipping had the emblems of mourning prominently displayed, while in many instances crowds occupied the rigging, and watched with mournful earnestness the little craft which carried upon its deck the remains of the nation's murdered Chief Magistrate. All the docks in the vicinity were filled with spectators.

Thousands thronged to the extreme verge of the piers and watched with breathless curiosity the movements of the "Jersey City" as she neared her destination. When within a few hundred yards of the dock, the German societies commenced a funeral ode which produced a thrilling effect upon all who heard it.

The scene at the foot of Desbrosses street could not fail to make a lasting impression upon the thousands who were congregated on the housetops and awnings for several blocks on each side of the ferry. Every available spot was occupied along Desbrosses street, from West to Hudson streets. The window sashes of all the houses were removed in order that the occupants might have an unobstructed view of the procession, and as far as the eye could see there was a dense mass of heads protruding from every window of the street.

Arrival of the Remains at Desbrosses Street Ferry

FROM VALENTINE

The route was from Desbrosses street through Hudson to Canal street, thence to Broadway and down Broadway to the City Hall. The escort marched in files on each flank of the funeral car. Then came the rest of the procession according to the programme. After them came the people by thousands, in solemn and orderly demeanor, from Desbrosses and Hudson streets in a vast throng, following in the rear and reaching from curb to curb on Canal street. This column increased as it went, and, with uncovered heads and steadily persistent steps, followed the remains of the lamented Chief Magistrate.

Hours before the arrival of the body, masses of people gathered in City Hall park, along Broadway and Chatham street and in and on the buildings overlooking the plaza, where the ceremony of receiving the body was to be witnessed. At the time of the appearance of the procession at the City Hall at least twenty thousand citizens were assembled.

The coffin was immediately taken from the hearse and carried up the stairs to the catafalque prepared for its reception, amid a solemn dirge, played by the Liederkranz band. The several German singing clubs, and numbering nearly a thousand voices, sang several solemn dirges.

Niche and dome, balustrade and panelling were all veiled. From the dome to the base there was a wall of crape. The light which fell upon the scene of death was modified. Across the oriels of the dome a black curtain was drawn, and the rays thus conducted fell subdued on the sad and imposing scene.

At the City Hall

ILLINOIS STATE HISTORICAL LIBRARY

THE NATION MOURNS.

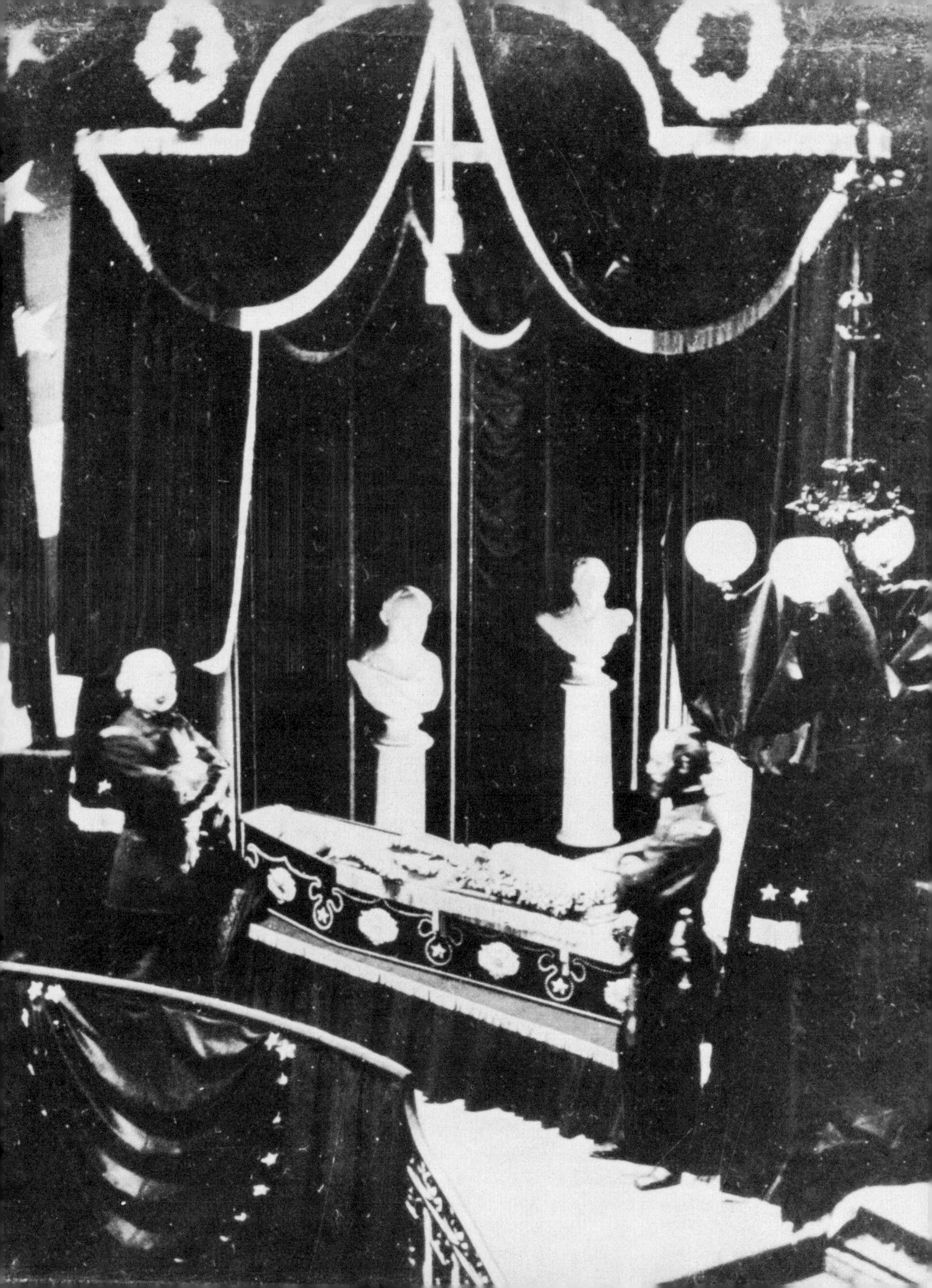

The catafalque graced the principal entrance to the Governor's Room. Its form was a square, but it was surmounted by a towering gothic arch, from which folds of crape, ornamented by festoons of silver lace and cords of tassels, fell artistically over the curtained pillars which gave form and beauty to the structure. The arch seemed lost in the dark labyrinths from which it rose.

The solemn procession commenced at one o'clock. Thousands formed that line. Throughout the long early summer day, into the cool hours of the evening, and away through the chilly hours of the night, till dawn was almost again breaking, the seemingly ever unbroken line of people kept its ground persistently—to gratify the earnest desire which had brought them together. But, notwithstanding the immense number which had passed during the day, the throng was at its greatest about midnight.

It was evident from the earliest hour that half those who were so patiently standing on the footpaths in Broadway and Centre street could not possibly get a view of the body within the time assigned. Still they remained in the ranks.

At twenty minutes to twelve o'clock (noon) the doors of admission were closed to the general public, and though for some hours past the people had been admitted at the rate of nearly one hundred a minute—and over one hundred and fifty thousand persons must have seen the body there yet remained immense crowds who were sent away disappointed.

FROM VALENTINE

As the clock tolled the hour of twelve, the members of the German singing societies commenced a solemn dirge.

ILLINOIS STATE HISTORICAL LIBRARY

The military formed chiefly on Broadway, and long before the procession moved the lines of soldiery extended from the City Hall the whole distance to Fourteenth street. In the narrow streets in the vicinity of the hall were arranged the component parts of the civic procession, and it seemed as if every court and alley was made the rallying point of some organization with its banner and long line of men in dark clothing.

NEW YORK HISTORICAL SOCIETY

NEW YORK HISTORICAL SOCIETY

The funeral car was an elegant piece of workmanship. The main platform was fourteen feet long, eight feet wide and fifteen feet in height. Above the dais was an elegant canopy, supported by four columns, and surmounted by a miniature Temple of Liberty. The platform was covered with black cloth, which fell at the sides nearly to the ground, and was edged with silver bullion fringe. The car was drawn by sixteen gray horses, covered with black cloth trimmings, each led by a groom.

The procession will move from the City Hall at one o'clock precisely, and will proceed up Broadway to Fourteenth street; through Fourteenth to Fifth avenue; up Fifth avenue to Thirty-fourth street; through Thirty-fourth to Ninth avenue, to the Hudson River Railroad depot.

LINCOLN NATIONAL LIFE FOUNDATION

ILLINOIS STATE HISTORICAL LIBRARY

The time appointed was one o'clock, but the hour hand pointed to two o'clock before it slowly marched off with steady, solemn pace, amid muffled roll of drums and saddened strains of funeral dirges from a number of bands. This procession was the grandest—the most imposing ever organized in the United States. It embraced military and civic associations representing all the lines of service, and all the various walks of official and business life.

When the gilded top of the temple surmounting the hearse was seen in the distance there was a general pushing and crowding in the dense throng on the sidewalks. At its nearer approach a simultaneous hush seemed to come over the entire crowd, and all eyes were fastened on the hearse and coffin from the time of its appearance till it passed out of sight.

It is estimated that there were in the procession one hundred thousand men, of whom twenty thousand were soldiers. One hundred bands sent forth solemn strains of music during the march. From half a million to a million spectators are supposed to have witnessed the spectacle. It occupied about four hours in passing any given point.

CARTER

TRIUMPHAL MARCH OF ABRAHAM LINCOLN

Rome in the palmiest days of its power never witnessed such a triumphal march as New York yesterday formed and looked upon. When four years ago Abraham Lincoln passed through the city to be armed with authority as the nation's leader, Broadway sufficed to contain the crowd which, with varied sentiments, cheered, and scoffed, and scowled him a doubtful welcome. When yesterday the same people, inspired with a common, universal sorrow, sadly followed his body, crowned with more glorious honors as the nation's savior, the same wide street held hardly a fraction of them.

Then he was going to be crowned chief magistrate of a divided people and disrupted nation on the eve of a great, bloody and uncertain war. Yesterday he was the great martyr of a nation united under his guidance and that of God, by the successful close of that gloomy war.

Then he passed through almost unknown, and the crowd that followed his coach with cheers were actuated by curiosity as much as admiration. Yesterday it was different; yesterday witnessed the real triumphal march of Abraham Lincoln; for he had conquered the prejudices of all hordes and classes, and the hearts of the people who honored him beat with love and veneration of the man.

Better for his fame that it should come thus late than too soon. The test of his success and his greatness can never be doubted or disputed.

NEW YORK HISTORICAL SOCIETY

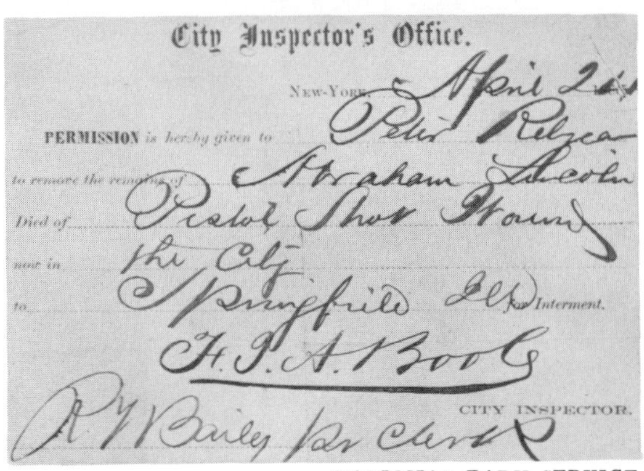

City Inspector's Office.

New-York, April 24

PERMISSION is hereby given to Peter Relyea

to remove the remains of Abraham Lincoln

Died of Pistol Shot Wound

now in the City

to Springfield Ill for Interment.

F. I. A. Boole

CITY INSPECTOR.

R. W. Bailey per Clerk

NATIONAL PARK SERVICE

At three o'clock, the head of the procession having reached the Hudson River Railroad depot in Twenty-ninth street between Ninth and Tenth avenues, the column halted to allow the hearse and escort to pass. At half-past three the approach of the hearse was made known by the solemn refrains of the bands and the muffled roll of martial drums. When the head of the procession reached the station the rear of it had not passed Fourteenth street. When the train containing the body started from the depot at 4:15, the procession was still progressing up Broadway.

The line of the Hudson River road seemed alive with people. At each of the towns by which it passed, the darkness of the night was relieved by torches, which revealed the crowds there assembled. At Hudson, where the train arrived at midnight, elaborate preparations had been made. Beneath an arch hung with black and white drapery and evergreen wreaths was a tableau representing the coffin resting on a dais; a female figure in white, mourning over the coffin. While a band of young women dressed in white sang a dirge, two others in black entered the funeral-car, placed a floral device on the President's coffin. This whole scene was one of the most weird ever witnessed, its solemnity being intensified by the somber lights of torches, at that dead hour of the night. MAJOR GENERAL TOWNSEND.

NATIONAL PARK SERVICE

At Sing Sing there was an immense assemblage. The train passed under an arch eighteen feet from base to base, made of alternate strips of black and white muslin, and the verges covered with black velvet.

ALBANY

Arrive Tuesday, April 25, 11 P.M.
Leave Wednesday, April 26, 4 P.M.

The Funeral ceremonies of yesterday will long be remembered. The remains of the lamented President had been placed in the Assembly Chamber, and during the still hours of the early morning, a sad procession moved through our streets to and from the Capitol. Aside from the slow tread of this procession, not a sound was to be heard in the streets, and never upon a Sabbath morning did the city present a stillness so complete.

The procession formed in double file, reached from the Capitol to Broadway, slowly and patiently moving. All forenoon the trains and excursion boats brought large numbers from the surrounding country, many coming from distances of two hundred miles.

From one in the morning, until two in the afternoon, a stream of people passed through the Capitol and yet thousands were still waiting their turns when the hour for closing the coffin arrived. It is estimated that not less than fifty thousand visited the remains. Soon after two the procession commenced to move, the Bands playing "Love Not," "Auld Lang Syne," "Come and Let Us Worship"; the effect was thrilling.

The hearse, with the coffin resting in an elegant and elaborately finished Catafalque, trimmed with white silk, adorned richly with silver mountings, and surmounted by the Eagle, was drawn by eight white horses.

I had charge, in my official capacity as Secretary of State, of the train after it left Albany. The train was running all night through central and western New York. Wherever the highway crossed the railroad track the whole population of the neighborhood was assembled on the highway and in the fields. Huge bonfires lighted up the scene. Pastors of the local churches of all denominations had united in leading their congregations for greeting and farewell to their beloved President. As we would reach a crossing there sometimes would be hundreds and at others thousands of men, women and children on their knees, praying and singing hymns. The continuous service of prayer and supplication lasted over the three hundred miles between Albany and Buffalo, from midnight until dawn. CHAUNCEY DEPEW.

BUFFALO & ERIE COUNTY HISTORICAL SOCIETY

BUFFALO & ERIE COUNTY HISTORICAL SOCIETY

It consists of a broad platform, valanced to the very ground with black velvet; in its centre an elevated rest for the coffin, the whole surmounted by a temple-formed canopy, with black plumes at its apex and large rosettes of white crape at the corners. The entire draping of the car is of rich black velvet with heavy silver fringing. It was drawn as before, by six magnificent white horses, housed to the feet in black, each led by a colored groom.

BUFFALO
Arrive Thursday, April 27, 7:00 A.M.
Leave Thursday, April 27, 10:10 P.M.

The solemn spectacle has passed. The body of the great martyr has been borne through our hushed streets, and onward to rest. We have looked upon the immortal face, and a sacred memory is in our hearts. The august procession of the cities and states has swept on to the West, and the funeral dirge which wailed up to us from the ocean a week ago is dying along the lakes. What a journey of the dead it is that we have seen!

At ten minutes before seven, the pilot engine arrived to announce the approach of the funeral train. Punctually to the time the latter came slowly in—so slowly and silently, that it announced by its very manner the solemnity of its nature. The procession in point of numbers and magnitude, lacked very much in comparison with the procession of last week, but it had the deep solemnity of a real funeral over a fictitious ceremony. The crowd in the vicinity of St. James Hall, through the forenoon, was terrible, and we heard of many cases of fainting on the part of the ladies.

As the remains were placed upon the dais the St. Cecelia Society sang the solemn dirge, "Rest, Spirit, Rest," with impressive effect and coming through the folds of the drapery the sweet strains of melody seemed, indeed, angelic. The marching through the courts of death was as ceaseless as the flow of mighty waters. All day long did the stream pass along uninterruptedly. It is safe to estimate the total number of people that passed through during the day, at from eighty to one hundred thousand.

At half past eight o'clock the procession moved toward the depot. The bands played solemn dirges, and with the darkness of the night all was wrapped in deepest gloom. At a little after ten o'clock the funeral cortege took the train and went their sorrowful way to the west.

CLEVELAND

Arrive Friday, April 28, 7:20 A.M.
Leave Friday, April 28, Midnight.

By day-break the streets were alive with people. Bands, playing slow music and solemn airs, passed along the streets. At an early hour every road leading to the city was thronged with vehicles. The whole surrounding country emptied itself into Cleveland. Special trains were run on all the railroads. The funeral train arrived at Euclid street station at 7:20 A.M. As it approached a national salute of thirty-six guns was fired.

As the magnificent cortege moved slowly and solemnly down Euclid street, led by the band playing a funeral march, the vast crowd of both sexes and of all ages and conditions, eager and reverent spectators of the grand pageant, began a general movement down the broad beautiful avenue. The vast multitude who lined the streets fell into line in the rear and the monster procession moved on to the solemn beat of funeral music, stretching its length full two miles through the beautiful avenue.

From actual count by several gentlemen, the average number passing through the temple may be placed at one hundred forty a minute. A total of about 65,000 saw the remains.

As early as seven o'clock a large concourse had assembled at the Square and steadily the multitude was swelled until far back from the ropes a forest of humanity stood expectant.

The hearse was drawn by six pure white horses, all appropriately decorated, and each attended by a colored groom wearing badges of mourning.

At ten o'clock the embalmer fastened down the lid of the coffin. The night was black as ink, and the rain fell in torrents, forbidding the grand demonstration that was contemplated. A platoon of policemen headed the procession, bearing lamps.

Large numbers of men and women, with or without shelter, accompanied the cortege. The wet streets glistening in the gas and torchlight, the rain pouring in deluges, the lamps swaying and flaring in the air, the bands playing mournful funeral marches and wailing dirges—nothing could so blanch the cheek and chill the blood, no spectacle could be more weird. The cortege left the temple at half past ten and moved to the funeral train.

The train soon after moved off over the road to Columbus, and will arrive at the Capital City at half past seven this morning.

Pickpockets—The police force had a lively time yesterday with the light-fingered fraternity which was largely represented here. A number of the latter were "spotted" and locked up. A number of cases came to our knowledge, of persons who were relieved of their scrip and greenbacks. Such things will happen in every great concourse of people, no matter how serious and solemn the occasion.

CHICAGO HISTORICAL SOCIETY

COLUMBUS

Arrive Saturday, April 29, 7:30 A.M.
Leave Saturday, April 29, 8:00 P.M.

Sorrow hung like a heavy pall over the whole city—an occasion never to be forgotten by those who witnessed the impressive scenes of the day, for Columbus seemed like one vast cenotaph. The funeral train came to a stop so the car bearing the President was placed directly in the center of High street. As the immense procession moved slowly down High street, sorrow was depicted upon the countenances of all.

As the cortege reached Broad street, a temporary halt was occasioned, and at this point the Hook and Ladder truck of the Fire Department elegantly draped and canopied, was an object of universal interest. Beneath this magnificent mourning canopy were seated forty-two young ladies, habited in deep mourning, who sang the 1027th Hymn of the M.E. collection. This sweet sacred music, blending with the sublime strains of Pleyel's German Hymn—the mingling of youthful voices with the brazen yet soft tones of the music of the military bands, added to the deep diapason of the minute-guns—produced an indescribable effect.

On this plane the coffin rested. The sides of the dais were lined with flowers and green sprigs, white roses, rose buds and myrtle. At each end stood a large urn filled with delicate flowers, and on each side of the dais was the word "LINCOLN."

ILLINOIS STATE HISTORICAL LIBRARY

OHIO HISTORICAL SOCIETY LIBRARY

About nine o'clock the advance of the procession arrived at the Capitol. The coffin was opened and the face of the deceased exposed to view. No whisper even resounded through the hours. It is estimated that by actual count over eight thousand persons passed in and out every hour, from half past nine A.M. until 4 o'clock and after making due allowances, it is estimated that over 50,000 viewed the remains.

The Band of the U.W. Infantry stationed on the west terrace of the Capitol discoursed most excellent music during the morning.

Long before two o'clock P.M. the entire space fronting the east terrace was crowded densely with people, who had gathered to hear the oration upon the life and death of the President. The Hon. Job Stevenson delivered the funeral oration. At the conclusion Gen. Hooker was called upon, who excused himself briefly, upon the grounds of its being in bad taste and inappropriate.

Shortly before six o'clock the body was borne to the funeral car at the west gate to the Capitol. The mourning emblems, the solemn dirges of the various military bands, the tolling of bells, and the heavy booming of artillery, together with the singing of Hymns from childrens' voices, swelled on the night air in one grand and appropriate requiem, was a fitting end to the solemnities of the day. At 8 o'clock the train bearing its precious freight left Columbus never to return.

LINCOLN NATIONAL LIFE FOUNDATION

INDIANAPOLIS
Arrive Sunday, April 30, 7:00 A.M.
Leave Sunday, April 30, 12 M.

The crowd present was the largest ever assembled in Indianapolis, and numbered not less than fifty thousand persons.

At 7 o'clock in the morning it commenced raining, and continued during the entire day, but notwithstanding, the streets were densely thronged with an eager, anxious mass of humanity willing to endanger fine apparel in order to behold what was to be seen. The manner in which dimity, once as spotless as the driven snow, loves of bonnets and gorgeous dresses were sacrificed was most reckless. All in all, the multitude presented the most grotesque and ridiculous appearance we have ever witnessed. Wet, tired, cold and famished, be-dabbled with mud and filth, they presented a sorry sight indeed. No more inclement and uncharitable day could have been, and no more enthusiastic mass of sight-seers could possible have collected together.

The order of the procession was formed with his excellency Gov. Morton and Major General Joseph Hooker on Horseback in front, after which came the funeral car, drawn by six white horses caparisoned in black cloth fringed with silver lace and led by grooms. The burial case could be plainly seen and is said to be the most magnificent ever constructed in this country. On account of the rain the procession that was intended did not come off, nor the delivery of the funeral oration.

At the south entrance to the State House campus, was erected out of heavy oak timber, a large canopy 30 by 40 feet and fifteen feet in height, surmounted by a frailer structure of twelve feet in height. The upper part was intended for the orator, bands and choir, but was not used. Under this the cortege passed as did all the procession. The whole work is finely gotten up.

Large bonfires at numerous points in the street shed a lurid glare, as the red flames leaped upwards towards the dark vault above, where still hung the threatening clouds that had for twelve hours poured their contents upon the unsheltered thousands below. At eleven o'clock the soldiers were again formed in lines extending on either side of the street, from the State House to the Union Depot, and at the distance of a few feet holding torches. The wailing sadness of the music, the fitful glare of the lamps, the deep silence unbroken except by the heavy tramp of the soldiers and muffled rumbling of the carriage wheels, made it the most impressive scene of all, in the mournful occasion.

The coffin was again deposited in the car, and at 12 midnight the train left for Chicago at which place it will arrive today. At the time we write (2 A.M.) the streets are deserted, and the mantle of night sets brooding where but a few hours since was witnessed the most solemn event that has ever occurred in the history of the nation.

LINCOLN NATIONAL LIFE FOUNDATION

And so it was with all the towns and villages.

Wellington, O. 2 A.M. The people from the surrounding country and villages assembled at the depot with anxious looks and wonder.

Greenwich, O. The rain is pouring down in torrents, and yet there is a large bonfire burning around which are grouped some two hundred people who stand uncovered.

Shelby, O. 3:30 A.M. A large crowd assembled with lighted lamps.

Galion, O. 4:23 A.M. The villagers and country people assembled and looked at the train.

Richmond, Indiana. 2 A.M. At least 5000 people are standing in the solemn gloom of midnight. As the train slowly passes under the arch, a tableau of the Goddess of Liberty weeping, while a brass band plays a dirge, adds greatly to the scene.

Cambridge City. 4:15 A.M. The train was received with salvos of artillery. The darkness was turned into a solemn glare by the burning of the Bengal lights. The effect was very impressive.

San Francisco,
Thursday, April 20, 1865

The funeral services in honor of the late President in this city yesterday were the grandest ever witnessed on the Pacific coast. The procession, three miles long, contained 15,000 people. The obsequies were observed in every town in the State, and in the principal towns of Nevada.

The Observance at San Francisco

THE COLLECTIONS OF THE SOCIETY OF CALIFORNIA PIONEERS

LINCOLN NATIONAL LIFE FOUNDATION

A Stop at Michigan City

At Michigan City

Spanning the track upon which the funeral train was to pass was a very handsome and elaborately decorated triple arch, twenty-four feet square at the base, and resting upon nine columns fourteen feet in height. The entire structure was beautifully trimmed with evergreens intertwined with alternate stripes of black and white muslin. On the arches were appropriate mottoes.

The most beautiful and interesting feature of the whole display was a congregation of young ladies and girls representing the different states, and the Goddess of Liberty. The states were represented by thirty-four young ladies dressed in white and wearing black sashes. The effect of the whole was beautiful.

The funeral train reached Michigan City at fifteen minutes before 8 o'clock. Immediately there came from the depot a solemn procession of eighteen ladies dressed in mourning, with black skirts and white waists, and wearing black sashes, bearing flowers which were to be laid on the coffin. Next in order came the young ladies representing the states of the union, who silently passed by the dead.

In a moment the crush around the cars became so furious that several were bodily borne down and trampled upon by those around them. All the efforts of the escort and guard of soldiers were required to be put forth to prevent a rush through the car. Men, women and children vied with each other in their wild and frantic efforts to enter the car. So great was the rush and confusion that several times it was announced that no more persons would be permitted to enter the train, and thousands were turned away sadly disappointed.

CHICAGO

Arrive Monday, May 1, 11 A.M.
Depart Tuesday, May 2, 9:30 P.M.

Heavy black clouds trailed in ragged masses over the face of the sky, and a bleak, cold wind shivered through the trees. But as the early hours wore on the sun began to pierce the overshadowing mist, and at 8 o'clock the air was bathed in warm sunshine. It was indeed a morning pure and sweet, peaceful and calm, such as the imagination always loves to dwell upon in connection with a pageant.

Between 8 and 9 o'clock a mighty tide of people might have been perceived flowing from all parts of the city towards Park place. There the body was to be received; there the gorgeous funeral arch was erected; and there were to be performed the most solemn and impressive rites which would be witnessed in the whole ceremony.

The Concourse at Park Place

Park place is a short avenue leading eastward from Michigan avenue, and commanding a fine prospect of the lake and all that portion of the city. It is perhaps the most picturesquely situated of any part of the city. Slowly the crowds began to collect round the spot. In a single hour an immense concourse had gathered. Far and near, the multitudes pressed on, along the avenue, along the shore, and over the railway track, uniting in one dense mass around the space apportioned to the reception ceremony. Then the housetops began to be alive with eager and expectant faces.

Before 10 o'clock the whole ground, from Park place as far as the eye could discern, was covered with one promiscuous sea of human beings that seemed to ebb and flow, and rise and fall, scattering its spray even to the tree tops. A sort of breathless suspense began to pervade the multitude. An impressive stillness prevailed, all eyes were stretched in the direction where the train would first come in sight. It was yet a full hour before the time when it was expected to arrive.

Arrival of the Funeral Escort

As the time drew near to 11 o'clock the impatience of the vast concourse began to grow more intense, all eyes were directed to the spot from which the long expected train was soon to emerge. Slowly it came into view, winding round the bend, and approaching with its dreary freight that anxious, upturned sea of human faces. The train paused in front of the arch, amid the same profound silence which had preceded its arrival.

FRANK LESLIE'S ILLUSTRATED NEWSPAPER, MAY 20, 1865

Receiving the Remains

The military guard of honor proceeded to take their appointed stations. Then the committee of one hundred citizens, who received the remains in Michigan City, descended from the cars. Another pause ensued, during which the excitement of the people became more and more intense. At length the coffin made its appearance, borne on the shoulders of eight sergeants of the guard, who proceeded slowly down the platform toward the funeral arch. The Great Western Light Guard band played a solemn air while the soldiers carried the coffin up the sloping platform erected in front of the arch, beneath which the funeral car was awaiting the remains.

IN PEACE NOBLE SOUL, PATRIOT
Faithful to Right. A Martyr to Justice

The Funeral Arch

Amid all the impatience and keen, though subdued, excitement which prevailed, there was one object to which attention was irresistibly directed, and which the people seemed never to tire in gazing upon. This was the gorgeous funeral arch, through which the remains were to pass. It was placed near the centre of Park place, spanning the entire width of the street, half way between Michigan avenue and the lake. It consisted of a triple gothic arch, spanning fifty-one feet and was sixteen feet deep. The centre arch was twenty-seven feet high and twenty-four feet wide. The mourning drapery was entwined around the arches up to the pinnacle in the centre—a height of forty feet. In the crown of the arch, on each side, appeared a bust of the president.

The Funeral Car

The funeral car, which formed the most imposing feature of the procession, had in itself a costly and magnificent appearance. The car was fourteen feet in length, eight feet wide and fifteen feet in height. On top of each pillar was a massive urn covered with black and white crape. From each corner over the urns drooped the American flag, partly furled and covered with crape, and on the centre of the roof was placed a large American stuffed eagle, which was recently shot in Michigan. The inside of the canopy was a deep blue tint. In the centre on each side was a black velvet background, on which appeared the name "Lincoln," in large letters. It was drawn by ten horses, each one led by a colored groom.

An Impressive Ceremony

After the coffin was placed upon the dais in the car, and while the solemn strains of the funeral march were pealing in the air, a most beautiful and touching rite was performed. This was the strewing of immortelles and garlands upon the bier, by thirty-six young ladies of the high school. Before the arrival of the funeral escort this fair company of maidens had been the object of universal admiration and remark. Attired in snow white robes, with a simple sash of black crape tied with a rosette at the side, bare-headed and with black velvet wreaths over their brows, in front of which sparkled a single star—they looked the very emblems of purity. It seemed as if a troop of snowy doves had suddenly fluttered down from heaven with messages of peace to men.

LIBRARY OF CONGRESS

HARPER'S WEEKLY, MAY 20, 1865

CHICAGO HISTORICAL SOCIETY

CHICAGO HISTORICAL SOCIETY

The last of the procession passed through the court-house at 4 o'clock, and the preparations for the lying-in-state were proceeded with. At six the doors were opened, and a continual crowd began to pour into the rotunda, which did not cease during the entire night. All gazed intently at the features of one whom so many had known so well in life.

The body will lie in state all day in the court-house. Shortly before 7 o'clock in the evening the coffin will be closed and the remains escorted to the depot by a torch-light procession.

And when it was night, and the coffin was closed, and the young ladies came to place upon it fresh flowers, and the last dirge was being chanted by the choir, and the guard of honor and escorts surrounded the bier, and the coffin was borne upon the shoulders of the veteran sergeants to the hearse, between the lines of flaring torches—even then, when the gates of the public square had been closed for an hour, a long dense column still waited in vain.

CHAPTER V

I BID YOU AN AFFECTIONATE FAREWELL

HOME TO SPRINGFIELD

The Representative Hall

SKETCH BY W. WAUD, HARPER'S WEEKLY, MAY 27, 1865

The Draped State House ILLINOIS STATE HISTORICAL LIBRARY

Springfield, Illinois
April 30, 1865

The people are all very busy making preparations for the funeral on Thursday the 4th. They are draping the State House inside and out, and the big columns are covered with evergreen from bottom to top. They sent to Michigan for pines, and they have wagon loads of black goods.

The people have bought the Mather grounds in the heart of the city six acres for a burial place. It is a beautiful grove of native trees. They got it for $5300.00 and have a vault nearly finished, but last night Mrs. Lincoln telegraphed that she would not let him be buried there. The people are in a rage about it and all the hard stories that ever were told about her are told again. She has no friends here.

Yours affectionately, H.P.H. Bromwell.

ILLINOIS STATE HISTORICAL LIBRARY

The Unfinished Tomb

There was left to us the little sign that had hung outside the narrow stairway entrance to the office, and that had been there with its inviting welcome to friend and foe alike for twenty-one years. None of us was prepared for the startling shock that came when black drapery covered and darkened that familiar entrance and office front on the terrible morning following America's darkest night of April 14, 1865.

HERBERT GEORG STUDIO, INC. *The Lincoln-Herndon Law Office*

The first task to which we were assigned was to drape Lincoln's home in mourning. I being slender and about sixteen years of age, was told to put the droopers on the eaves of the house and to fasten the droopers with rosettes about eight feet apart. I was let down the roof on a rope. Mrs. Tilton came to the window near where I was working and told me to be sure to get them eight feet apart. I replied I could hardly do so, as I was lying on my stomach and could not gauge the distance. She went and procured a two-foot rule, passing it down to me with the remark she had taken it from Lincoln's old desk, and I could keep it when I had completed my task.

Mrs. Lincoln made up her mind that Oak Ridge was the only place she desired or would consent to. Then the trouble began. Seats had to be built for the choir, and we all hurried off to the cemetery to erect the seats. The choir of three hundred voices must be provided for. We had to work two days and one night to complete the work.

The house was then occupied by Mr. Tilton, president of the Great Western Railroad, and his family very kindly showed the strangers through the rooms made sacred by Lincoln's presence and use. Finally, however, the crowds became so numerous, it was found necessary to place a guard around the house to prevent depredations. Permission had been given the visitors to carry away a leaf or a flower as a souvenir, but many were not content with this and chipped off pieces of the fence, and one man was caught in the act of carrying away a brick from the wall.

ILLINOIS STATE HISTORICAL LIBRARY

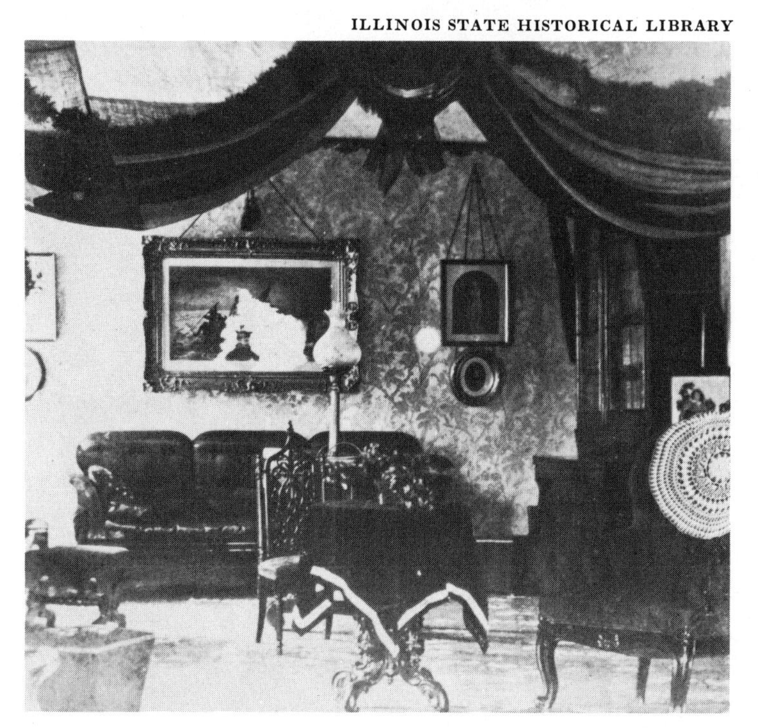

The Parlor

ILLINOIS STATE HISTORICAL LIBRARY

The President's House

Large numbers visited the former home of the late President, at the corner of Eighth and Jackson streets. The delegation of one hundred from Chicago had their photographs taken as a memorial of the solemn occasion.

ILLINOIS STATE HISTORICAL LIBRARY

Two locomotives were assigned, one to draw the train proper, the other to act as "pilot." At all the larger places, like Joliet, Wilmington, Bloomington and Lincoln, there were large crowds congregated—stern, grim visaged men, tear bedimmed women and children—all silent, but with an anxious, expectant look, as of some impending disaster. There were throngs of people at all the smaller towns, also at the country road crossings could be seen a group of people waiting to see the train, remembrance of which was to become an epoch in their lives.

Long previous to the arrival of the remains, crowds of people numbering thousands were gathered at the Alton and Chicago Railroad depot, and along the lines for long distances. Every building and house top was covered with anxious and solemn men. The train did not make its appearance until a few minutes before nine. When the "pilot engine" draped in mourning made its appearance, the feelings of the crowd were intense, but only manifested by the almost breathless silence. After the procession had been formed it proceeded to the State House.

ILLINOIS STATE HISTORICAL LIBRARY

Chicago and Alton Railroad Company.

TIME TABLE

FOR THE SPECIAL TRAIN, CONVEYING THE FUNERAL CORTEGE WITH THE REMAINS OF THE LATE

PRESIDENT

FROM

CHICAGO TO SPRINGFIELD,

Tuesday, May 2, 1865.

[illegible]	[illegible]			
		CHICAGO	Leave	9:30 P. M.
1.7	1.7	FORT WAYNE JUNCTION	"	9:45 "
3.5	1.8	BRIDGEPORT	"	9:55 "
12.0	8.5	SUMMIT	"	10:25 "
17.6	5.0	JOY'S	"	10:40 "
25.5	8.0	LEMONT	"	11:10 "
32.5	7.0	LOCKPORT	"	11:30 "
37.7	5.2	JOLIET	"	11:50 "
46.4	8.7	ELWOOD	"	12:18 A. M.
48.6	2.3	HAMPTON	"	12:27 "
53.0	4.5	WILMINGTON	"	12:42 "
58.0	4.8	STEWART'S GROVE	"	12:58 "
61.4	3.5	BRACEVILLE	"	1:08 "
65.0	3.8	GARDNER	"	1:22 "
74.0	9.0	DWIGHT	"	1:52 "
82.0	8.0	ODELL	"	2:17 "
87.4	5.2	CAYUGA	"	2:35 "
92.3	5.0	PONTIAC	"	2:52 "
97.8	5.6	OCOYA	"	3:09 "
102.6	4.7	CHENOA	"	3:25 "
110.6	8.0	LEXINGTON	"	3:52 "
118.5	7.9	TOWANDA	"	4:18 "
124.0	5.7	ILL. CENTRAL R. R. JUNCTION	"	4:37 "
126.0	2.0	BLOOMINGTON	"	4:43 "
133.0	6.8	SHIRLEY	"	5:07 "
136.5	3.6	FUNK'S GROVE	"	5:18 "
141.4	4.8	McLEAN	"	5:35 "
146.0	4.8	ATLANTA	"	5:50 "
150.0	4.0	LAWN DALE	"	6:03 "
156.8	6.7	LINCOLN	"	6:26 "
164.0	7.1	BROADWELL	"	6:50 "
167.6	3.7	ELKHART	"	7:03 "
173.5	5.9	WILLIAMSVILLE	"	7:22 "
178.3	4.8	SHERMAN	"	7:38 "
180.0	2.1	SANGAMON	"	7:46 "
185.0	5.0	SPRINGFIELD	Arrive	8:00 "

The following instructions are to be observed for the above train:

1. All other Trains on this Road must be kept thirty minutes out of the way of the time of this Train.
2. All Telegraph Stations must be kept open during the passage of this Train.
3. A Guard with one red and one white light will be stationed at all road crossings by night; and with a white flag draped by day, or after day-light, on Wednesday morning.
4. A Pilot Engine will run upon this time, which is to be followed by the Funeral Train, ten minutes behind.
5. Pilot Engine must not pass any Telegraph Station, unless a white flag by day, or one red and one white light by night, shall be exhibited, which will signify that the Funeral Train has passed the nearest Telegraph Station. In the absence of said signals, the Pilot Engine will stop until definite information is received in regard to the Funeral Train.
6. The Funeral Train will pass all Stations slowly, at which time the bell of the Locomotive must be tolled.

By order of Brevet Brigadier General D. C. McCallum, 2d Div., in charge of Military Railroads.

ROBERT HALE,
General Superintendent.

The casket was placed in the Representative Hall—the very chamber in which in 1854 the deceased had pronounced that fearful invective against the sin of slavery. The doors were thrown open, and the coffin lid was removed, and we who had known the illustrious dead in other days and before the nation lay its claim upon him, moved sadly through and looked for the last time on the silent upturned face of our departed friend.

All day long and through the night a stream of people filed reverently by the catafalque. Some of them were his colleagues at the bar; some his old friends from New Salem; some crippled soldiers fresh from the battlefield of the war; some were little children who, scarce realizing the impressiveness of the scene, were destined to live and tell their children yet to be born the sad story of Lincoln's death.

WILLIAM H. HERNDON,
Lincoln's law partner.

All night long the tramping of feet was heard upon the pavement as the weary night watches wore away. In addition to the numbers present on Wednesday, the several railroads brought to the city yesterday many thousands of persons, and ere it was light the throng was passing in long columns towards the Representative Hall.

It is estimated that seventy-five thousand persons—passed into the Hall. During the morning minute guns were fired, which added much to the solemnity of the scene. Every class was represented.

ILLINOIS STATE HISTORICAL LIBRARY *People Entering the State House*

OBSEQUIES OF PRESIDENT LINCOLN

ORDER OF FUNERAL PROCESSION.

The Committtee on Ord r of Procession, have adopted the following order of Funeral Procession:

ORDER OF FUNERAL PROCESSION
OF
ABRAHAM LINCOLN,
Late President of the United States.

Under the immediate direction of Major General Joseph Hooker, Marshal in Chief.

Brig. Gen. John Cook and Staff.

Brevet Brig. Gen. James Oakes and Staff.

MILITARY.

FUNERAL ESCORT.

FIRST DIVISION.

Col. C. M. Prevost, 16th Regiment V. R. C., Marthal.

Aids—Lieut. Thomas B. Beach, A. A. A. General, Major Horace Holt, 1st Massachusetts Heavy Art., Capt. J. C. Reunison, 15th N.Y. Cavalry, Capt. E. C. Ray-
~~mond, 106th Ill. Infantry, Capt. Eddy, 95th Ill.~~
Inftry., Lieut. H. N. Schlick, 1st New York Dragoons.

To consist of Cavalry, Artillery and Infantry.

SECOND DIVISION.

Major F. Bridgeman, Pay Department U. S. A., Marshal.

Aids—Major R. W. McClaughry, Major W. W. White.

Officers and Enlisted Men of the Army and Navy, not otherwise assigned, in the order stated.

Officers in Uniform and Side Arms.

Major General John A. McClernand, Grand Marshal.

Aids—Lieut. Col. A. Schwartz, Capt. Henry Jayne, Capt. R. Rudolph, Capt. Benj. Ferguson, Thos. Owen, Hon. Charles [illegible], J. L. Million, Wm. M. Springer, [illegible] E. Myers, A. N. J. Crook, Ed. L. Merritt and N. Higgins.

THIRD DIVISION.

Col. Dudley Wickersham, 1st Army Corps, Marshal.

Aids—Joshua Rogers, Isaac A. Hawley, W. F. Kimber, J. B. Perkins and Charles Canfield.

Marshals of Sections—Col. William S. Barnum, Capt. A. J. Allen, Col. S. N. Hitt, C. L. Conkling, Robert P. Officer, Capt. T. G. Ba nes, D. W. Smith.

Officiating Clergymen.

Surgeons and Physicians of the Deceased.

Guard of Honor.

PALL BEARERS.
HEARSE.
PALL BEARERS.

Horse of the late President, led by two grooms.

Mourners.

Family of the Deceased.

FOURTH DIVISION.

Col. Speed Butler, Marshal.

Aids—Major Robert Allen, Capt. L. Rosette and Capt. Albert Williams.

Marshals of Sections—William E. Bennett, Hany W. Ives, Philip C. Latham, William V. Roll, K. H. Richardson, J. E. Williams and J. D. Crabb.

Civil authorities of the United States according to their relative dignities.

Foreign Ministers.

Civil authorities of the States and Territories, and of the District of Columbia, in the order stated, and according to their dignity in said order.

FIFTH DIVISION.

Hon. George L. Huntington, Marshal.

Aids—Dr. S. Babcock, George Shepherd, Charles Ridgley, George Latham, Moses B. Condell.

Municipal authorities of the city of Springfield and other cities.

SIXTH DIVISION.

Hon. William H. Herndon, Marshal.

Aids—P. P. Enos, C. S. Zane, T. W. Dresser, M. D.; John T. Jones, William G. Cochran, James Raybourne, Charles Vincent, Edward Beach, John Peters, C. W. Rearden, R. C. Huskey.

Marshals of Sections—Thomas Lyon, B. T. Hill, George Birge, Henry Yeakel, Jacob Halfen, —— Sweet, Dewitt C. Hartwell, Hamilton Hovey, Frederick B. Smith.

Members of the Christian, Sanitary, and other kindred Commissions.

Delegations from Bodies Politic, Universities and Colleges.

Clergy.

Members of the Legal Profession.

Members of the Medical Profession.

Representatives of the Press.

SEVENTH DIVISION.

Hon. Harman G. Reynolds, Marshal.

Aids—George R. Teasdale, John A. Hughes, James Smith, P. Fitzpatrick, Henry Shuck, Thomas O'Conner.

Marshals of Sections—Capt. Charles Fisher, Frank W. Tracy, M. Connor, Frederick Smith, M. Armstiong, Richard Young.

Free Masons.

Odd Fellows and other Fraternities.

Firemen.

EIGHTH DIVISION.

Hon. John W. Smith, Marshal.

Aids—Capt. Isaac Keye, S. H. Jones, Hon. John W. Priest, O. H. Abel, Henry N. Alden, Wm. P. Crafton, G. A. Kimber, John W. Poorman, Henry Ridgely, J. H. Crow, John W. Davis, Presco Wright, N. V. Hunt, George Dalbey, Alfred A. North, John S. Bradford, Samuel P. Townsend.

Citizens at large.

Colored Persons.

FORMATION AND MOVEMENT.

MILITARY.

First Division will form on the north side of Washington street, and fronting the Capitol Square.

Second Division on Washington street, right resting on the First Division.

Third Division on Washington street, right resting on the Second Division.

Fourth Division on North Fourth street, right resting on Washington street.

Fifth Division on North Fifth street, right resting on Washington street.

Sixth Division on North Sixth street, right resting on Washington street.

Seventh Division on North Seventh street, right resting on Washington street.

Eighth Division on North Eighth street, right resting on Washington street.

Divisions from Fourth to Eighth, inclusive, will form in the order stated, faced to the south.

Bands accompanying orders, societies, fraternities, delegations, &c., &c., will be permitted to accompany their respective bodies, &c., to the point designated as their position in the funeral column. After the formation they will be assigned such places as the Committee on Music may direct.

The procession will move from Washington to Eighth street; thence south to Monroe street; thence west to Fourth street; thence directly to Oak Ridge Cemetery.

Orders, societies, fraternities, delegations, &c., are requested to appear in the order prescribed above, and to walk eight abreast, and sections in close order. Marshals will strictly enforce this direction.

No carriages or vehicles will be allowed in the procession except the funeral car and carriages containing the family of the deceased.

The Marshal in Chief, Grand Marshals, Marshals of Divisions, and their Aids, Marshals of Sections, and the Guard of Honor, will be mounted—all others will move on foot.

On the first and third days of May thirteen guns will be fired at dawn, and afterwards at intervals of thirty minutes, between the rising and setting sun, a single gun, and at the close of the day a national salute of thirty-six guns.

On the fourth day of May, twenty-one guns at dawn, and afterwards single guns at intervals of ten minutes, until the procession moves; firing then will cease until the close of the day, when national salute of thirty-six guns will be fired.

Marshals will be designated by the following sashes and scarfs:

Grand Marshal—Red, White and Blue Sash.
Aids to the Grand Marshal—Red, White and Blue Scarf.
Marshals—Red Scarf.
Aids—Blue Scarf.

Marshals of Sections—White Scarf, the same to be draped with a black rosette on the right shoulder, and tied with crape on the left side.

The procession will move on Thursday, the 4th inst., at 10 o'clock A. M., precisely.

The streets through which the procession will pass must be kept clear from sidewalk to sidewalk.

JOHN. COOK,
Brig. Gen. Comd'g Dist. of Ill.
JAMES OAKES,
Brevet Brig. Gen. U. S. A.
JOHN A. McCLERNAND,
Grand Marshal.

ILLINOIS STATE HISTORICAL LIBRARY

(On the opposite page)
Waiting to Enter the State House
ILLINOIS STATE HISTORICAL LIBRARY

YATES AND SON.
F. GEORGE & SON.

ILLINOIS STATE HISTORICAL LIBRARY

Tendered by the Mayor of St. Louis to Mayor Dennis of this city, it is probably the most beautifully designed and finished carriage of the kind in the Western country. From the body springs silver pillars with gold base and capitals; each pillar is surmounted with a heavy bunch of ostrich feathers. The hearse was drawn by six superb black horses, richly draped and bearing on crests bunches of ostrich plumes.

And "Old Bob," the family horse, occupying a conspicuous place in the funeral procession, led by two grooms and caparisoned with velvet cloth. He had been sold sometime previously, and had been used as a drayhorse, until the assassination, when he was purchesed by two speculators, with the intention of showing throughout the country.

ILLINOIS STATE HISTORICAL LIBRARY

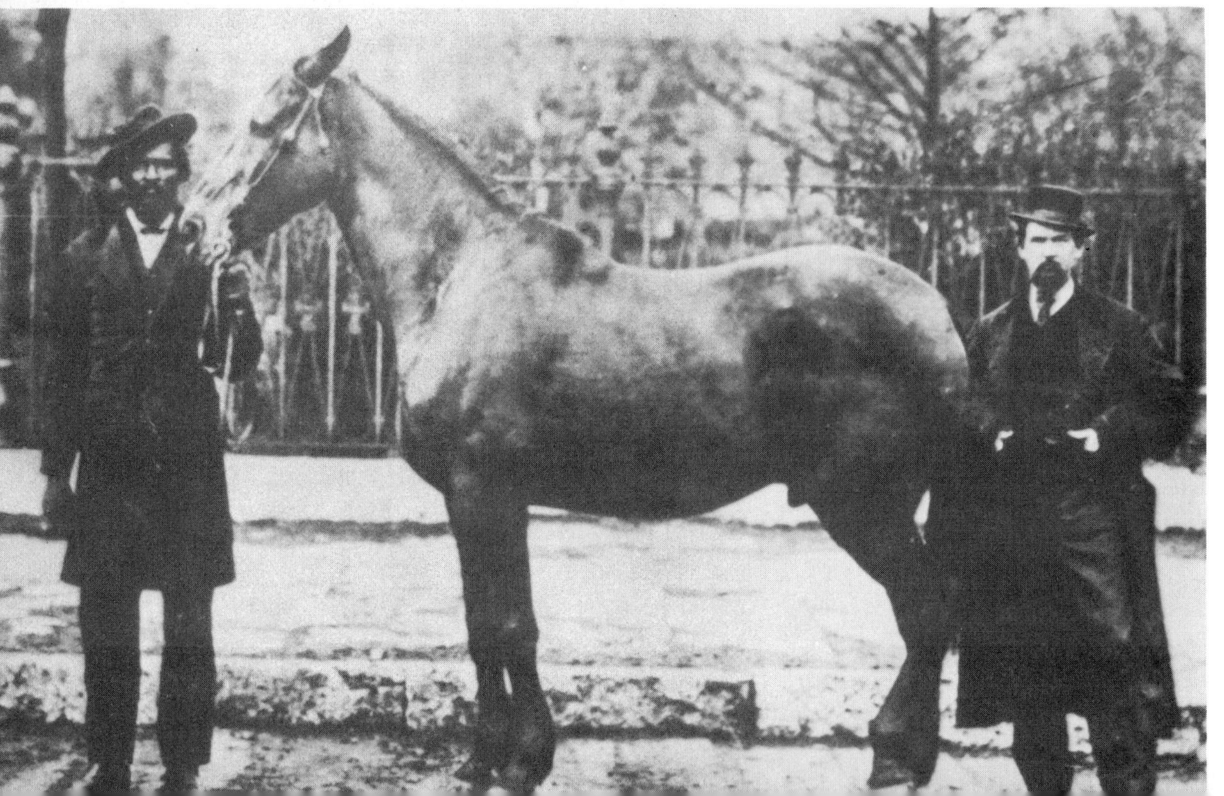

LINCOLN NATIONAL LIFE FOUNDATION

Forming the Procession

ILLINOIS STATE HISTORICAL LIBRARY

Oak Ridge very appropriately takes its name from two high ridges, running east and west, covered principally with large oak trees. Between these is a valley about seventy-five feet in depth, winding with pleasant irregularity, and watered by a little brook of clear water. The gate of the cemetery is at the head of this valley, and for several rods it descends quite rapidly, though near the tomb it is nearly level.

The tomb stands on the south side in a little cove in the bank, where it is quite steep, so that the roof of it is but a few feet in length. It is built of Joliet limestone, the architecture of the main arch is rustic. The upper range of the arch, projecting a few inches from the main wall, is of rubbed stone, and rests on Doric pilasters. The whole is about twelve feet high and ten wide.

*"A little more than four years ago,
from his plain and quiet home in yonder city,
he started . . ."*

Bishop Matthew Simpson

ILLINOIS STATE HISTORICAL LIBRARY

At about 10 o'clock A.M. the coffin was closed and the beloved features were shut out from the people forever. While these preparations were being made, a choir consisting of two hundred and fifty singers, and Lebrun's Washington band, assembled on the steps of the Capitol and sang "Peace Troubled Soul." As the remains were being brought out, the choir sang "Pleyel's Hymn," "Children of the Heavenly King."

The funeral pageant was the largest and most imposing ever witnessed in the United States. It was made up of military, professional and about every known fraternal and civic organization, embracing eight divisions. All were afoot, except the marshals, their aids, and distinguished guests. The columns of marchers reached from curb to curb and in close order. Gen. Joseph E. Hooker was marshal in chief.

The cortege was of such great numbers and of so great a length that the head of the procession had reached Oak Ridge, before more than one-half of it was in line. In this march to the "City of the Dead," scores upon scores of the best musical organizations of the nation were in line, whose funeral dirges cadenced the great wail of a bereft people.

The closing ceremonies at Oak Ridge were quite simple and in accord with the plain life of him whose mortal remains were laid to rest. Prayer was offered by the Rev. Albert Hale of this city, followed with appropriate music, in which a chorus of hundreds of voices joined.

Bishop Simpson of the Methodist Church delivered a lengthy and strong funeral oration, fierce in its revengeful and invective denunciation of the southern rebellion leaders. Probably it was more so than would have met the approval of the dead, generous President, but this the times seemed to excuse.

After the benediction was pronounced by the Rev. P. D. Gurley, the vast assemblage of mourners dispersed, sorrowing.

FROM B. F. MORRIS' NATION'S TRIBUTE TO ABRAHAM LINCOLN

Oakridge Cemetery,
SPRINGFIELD,
ILLINOIS.
N
W
E
S

1. PLACE RESERVED FOR FINAL BURIAL.
2. VAULT WITH REMAINS OF THE LATE PRESIDENT.
3. VAULTS.
4. ENTRANCE GATE.
5. HOUSE.
6. GARDEN GROUND.

ILLINOIS STATE HISTORICAL LIBRARY

The People

Interior of the Tomb

CHAPTER VI

MONSTROUSLY EVIL PLOT

BOOTH & COMPANY

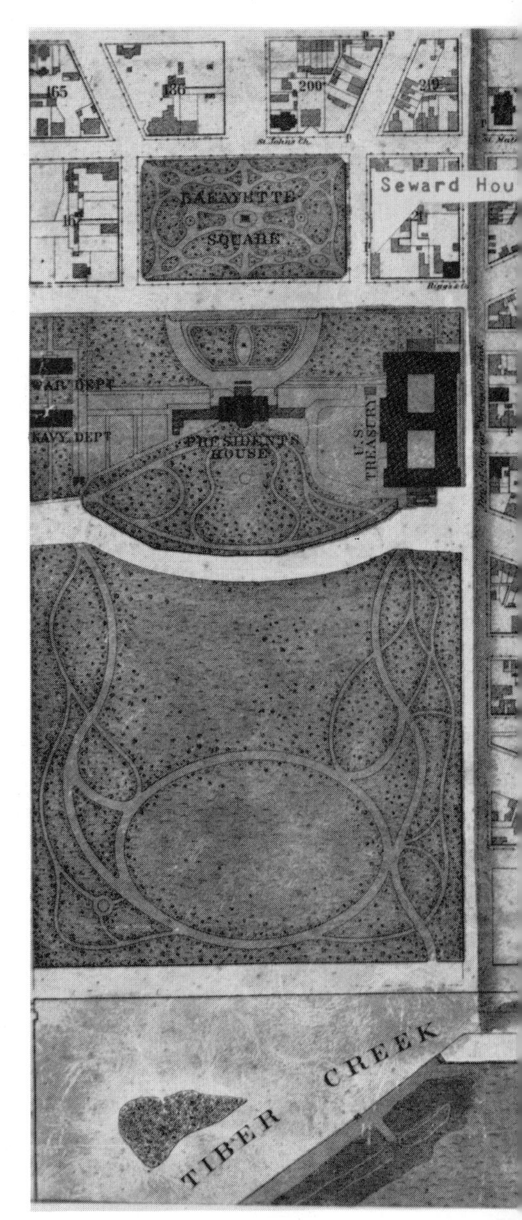

LIBRARY OF CONGRESS

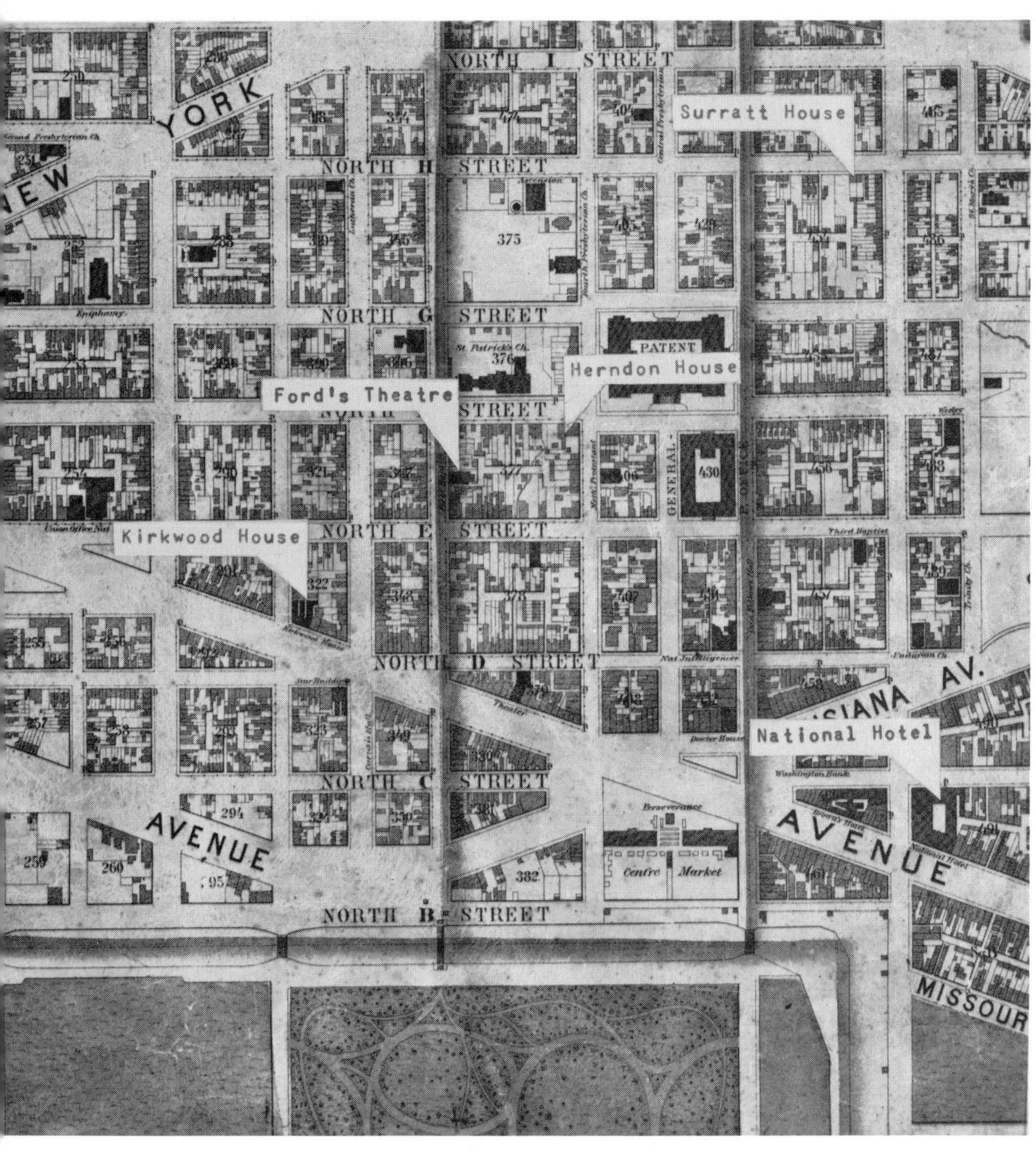

Map of Washington

There flashed before my mind the brilliant scene of the theater where in the past he had often appeared, with its lights, its music, its throngs of patrons, its gayety, all gathered to do honor to John Wilkes Booth.

He was, like many another brilliant man who has been overfond of his glass, one of the most charming of men. I think he was the most fascinating personality I have ever met in my long life. He was as handsome as a young god, with his clear, pale, olive complexion, classically regular features, and hair and mustache literally black as night; but his appearance was not more seductive than his manners. John Wilkes Booth cast a spell over most men with whom he came in contact, and I believe all women without exception.

That Booth was unquestionably laboring under some undue excitement was apparent to me a week before the fatal shot was fired. As I now clearly recall, he seemed to be crazed by some stress of inward feeling. As I afterwards remarked to friends when speaking of that experience, "Booth was crazy, but he didn't show it."

JOHN DEERY,
billiard-saloon owner.

—— 1864

"To whom it may concern."

Right or wrong, God judge me, not man. For be my motives good or bad, of one thing I am sure, the lasting condemnation of the North. I love peace more than life. To wait longer would be a crime. All hope for peace is dead. My prayers have proved as idle as my hopes. God's will be done. I go to see and share the bitter end.

The South can make no choice. It is either extermination or slavery for themselves (worse than death) to draw from. I know my choice.

I know how foolish I shall be deemed for taking such a step as this, where on the one side, I have many friends and many things to make me happy, where my profession alone has gained me an income of more than twenty thousand dollars a year, and where my great personal ambition in my profession has such a great field for labor.

A Confederate doing duty on his own responsibility.

J. WILKES BOOTH

John Wilkes Booth
NATIONAL ARCHIVES

Mrs. Surratt's House LIBRARY OF CONGRESS

SAMUEL ARNOLD
Following a period of service in the Confederate forces he returned to Baltimore where he was flattered to be remembered by his former schoolmate, the dashing Booth. He readily agreed to participate in the plan to abduct the President. Age twenty-eight.

LIBRARY OF CONGRESS

About the first of September 1864 J. Wilkes Booth sent word he would like to see me at Barnums Hotel in Baltimore. I had not seen Booth since 1852 at which time we were fellow Students of St. Timothys Hall, Cantonsville, Md. A tap at the door was given and O'Laughlin was ushered into the room. O'Laughlin was a former acquaintance of Booth's from boyhood up. We drank and freely conversed together about the war, the present condition of the South and in regard to the non-exchange of prisoners. Booth then spoke of the abduction or kidnapping of the President, saying if such could be accomplished, and the President taken to Richmond and held as a hostage, he thought it would bring about an exchange of prisoners. He said the President frequently went to the Soldiers Home, alone and unguarded, that he could be easily captured on one of these visits, and carried to the Potomac, boated across the river and conveyed to Richmond. Booth said he would furnish all the necessary materials to carry out the project. We consented to join him. SAMUEL ARNOLD.

In the fall of 1864 I was introduced to John Wilkes Booth who, I was given to understand, wished to know something about the main avenues leading from Washington to the Potomac. "In the Northern prisons are many thousands of our men

JOHN SURRATT
The younger son of Mary Surratt, he became at eighteen an agent for the Confederacy, "engaged in sending information regarding movements of the U. S. army at Washington and carrying dispatches to the Confederate boats on the Potomac." Age twenty-one.

LIBRARY OF CONGRESS

whom the United States government refuse to exchange. I have a proposition to submit to you, which I think if we can carry out will bring about the desired exchange." "Well sir, what is your proposition?" He then drew his chair close to me and in a whisper said, "It is to kidnap President Lincoln, and carry him off to Richmond." "Kidnap President Lincoln!" I said. I confess that I stood aghast at the proposition.

To think of successfully seizing Mr. Lincoln in the capital of the United States surrounded by thousands of soldiers, and carrying him off to Richmond, looked to me like a foolish idea. He went on to tell with what facility he could be seized in various rides to and from the Soldiers Home, his summer residence. He entered into the minute details of the proposed capture, and even the various parts to be performed by the actors in the performance. After two days reflection I told him I was willing to try it. JOHN SURRATT.

About the 15th of January I was passing down Seventh Street in company with Mr. Surratt, when someone called, "Mr. Surratt, Surratt!" and turning round Mr. Surratt recognized an old acquaintance, Dr. Samuel A. Mudd. Mr. Surratt introduced

Dr. Mudd to me; and Dr. Mudd introduced Mr. Booth, who was in company with him, to both of us. Booth invited us to his room at the National Hotel.

Dr. Mudd then went out into the passage and called Booth out and had a private conversation with him. Booth and Mudd came in and they called Surratt out. All three went out and had a private conversation. On returning Dr. Mudd apologized stating Booth and he had some private business. Booth at one time took out an envelope and made marks on it. I should not consider it writing but more in the direction of roads or lines.

LOUIS J. WEICHMANN.

On the night of the 15th of March about 12, Booth sent a messenger (Herold) requesting us to come to Gotiers Eating Saloon. Oysters, liquor, and cigars were obtained. Those present were the entire party who were concerned with the affair comprizing in all seven persons, viz. Jon. Wilkes Booth, John H. Surratt, Lewis Payne, George A. Atzerodt, David E. Herold, Michael O'Laughlin and myself. Booth opened the conversation setting forth his usual visionary idea contemplating the abduction from the Theatre. He and Payne were to seize him in the box, O'Laughlin to put out the gas, I was to jump on the stage and assist them as he was lowered down from the box. Surratt and Atzerodt alias Port Tobacco were to be on the other side

MICHAEL O'LAUGHLIN
A boyhood friend of Booth's from Baltimore, he and Arnold became the first recruits for the abduction scheme. After service in the Confederate army, he took the oath of allegiance and returned to Baltimore where he resumed his acquaintance with Booth. Age twenty-seven.

LIBRARY OF CONGRESS

of the Eastern Branch Bridge to act as pilots and to assist in conveying him to the boats which had been purchased by Booth.

I firmly objected to the whole scheme. I stated prisoners were now being exchanged. That I wanted a shadow of a chance for my life. An angry discussion arose between Booth and myself in which he threatened to shoot me. About 5 o'clock in the morning the meeting broke up.

On the 17th day of March 1865 about two o'clock Booth and Herold met O'Laughlin and myself. Booth stated the President was going to attend a theatrical performance at a soldiers Hospital at the outer edge of the city. SAMUEL ARNOLD.

We were instantly in our saddles on the way to the hospital. This was between one and two o'clock in the afternoon. It was our intention to seize the carriage, which was drawn by a splendid pair of horses and to have one of our men mount the box and drive direct for southern Maryland via Benning's bridge. We felt confident that all the cavalry in the city could never overhaul us. We were all mounted on swift horses, besides having a thorough knowledge of the country. By the time the alarm could have been given and horses saddled, we would have been on our way through southern Maryland towards the Potomac River. To our great disappointment, how-

DAVID HEROLD
The only son of his widowed mother, doubtless spoiled by his seven sisters, this weak-willed former pharmacist's clerk was a natural foil for the enchanting Booth. A boy in thought and deed, unstable and flighty, but valuable for his knowledge of roads and for his deep dedication to Booth. Age twenty-three.

LIBRARY OF CONGRESS

GEORGE ATZERODT

In seeking an unscrupulous character with knowledge of vehicles and southern Maryland roads Surratt found, among the dregs of Port Tobacco riff-raff, this carriage-maker turned blockade runner. Age thirty-three.

LIBRARY OF CONGRESS

ever, the President was not there but one of the government officials—Mr. Chase, if I mistake not. It was certainly a bitter disappointment. It was our last attempt. Accordingly, a separation finally took place. JOHN SURRATT.

During Payne's second visit to Mrs. Surratt's house, some time after the 4th of March, I returned from my office one day at half-past 4 o'clock. Dan, the negro servant, told me Massa John had left the house, with six others on horseback, about half past 2 o'clock. About half past 6 o'clock Surratt came in very much excited—in fact, rushed into the room. He had a revolver in his hand. I said, "John, what is the matter; why are you so much excited?" He replied, "I will shoot any one that comes into this room; my prospect is gone, my hopes are blighted; I want something to do; can you get me a clerkship?"

In about ten minutes after, the prisoner, Payne, came into the room. He was also very much excited, and I noticed he had a pistol. About fifteen minutes afterward, Booth came in so excited that he walked around the room three or four times very frantically, and did not notice me. LOUIS WEICHMANN.

LIBRARY OF CONGRESS

LEWIS PAYNE
(Lewis Thornton Powell)
A Confederate recruit at sixteen, he had fought on the Peninsula, at Antietam and Chancellorsville, had been wounded and captured in the Gettysburg charge, meanwhile acquiring a passion for killing and a monumental hatred for the Union. He was superbly suited to Booth's insanely conceived plot. Age twenty-one.

I am manager of Grover's Theater. On the day before the assassination he came into the office during the afternoon. He asked me if I intended to illuminate. He then asked, "Do you intend to" or "Are you going to invite the President?" My reply, I think, was, "Yes; that reminds me I must send that invitation." Booth's manner, and his entering in the way he did, struck me as rather peculiar. C. D. HESS.

On the 14th of April last, about half-past 11 o'clock my brother, James R. Ford told me that the President had engaged a box for that night. John Wilkes Booth was at the theater about half an hour afterward. I do not know that the fact of the President's going to the theater that night was communicated to Booth, but I think it is very likely he found it out while there. Three or four times during the season Booth had engaged box No. 7, that is part of the President's box, being the one nearest the audience. He engaged no other box. H. CLAY FORD.

Until today nothing was ever thought of sacrificing to our country's wrong. For six months we have worked to capture. FROM BOOTH'S DIARY.

The moment has at last arrived when my plans must be changed. The world may censure me for what I am about to do; but I am sure that posterity will justify me. Signed, Men who love their country better than gold or life.
JOHN WILKES BOOTH—PAYNE—ATZERODT, AND HEROLD.

On Friday, the day of the assassination I went to Howard's stable, having been sent there by Mrs. Surratt for the purpose of hiring a buggy. I drove her to Surrattsville the same day. Just before leaving the city, as I was going to the door, I saw Mr. Booth in the parlor, and Mrs. Surratt was speaking with him. They were alone. Immediately after he left, Mrs. Surratt and I started. LOUIS WEICHMANN.

I saw him that afternoon, sometime between two and four. Booth looked round, and said, "See what a nice horse I have got! Now watch: he can run just like a cat!" and he stuck spurs into the horse, and off he went down the street.

JAMES P. FERGUSON,
saloon keeper.

In the evening, between five and six o'clock, Booth came into the theater and asked me for a halter. I went out to the stable and put the halter on the horse. Booth, Maddox, "Peanut John," and myself went out to the adjoining restaurant next door, and took a drink at Booth's expense.

EDWARD SPANGLER,
stage carpenter.

On the evening of the 14th of April, I met Booth and Payne at the Herndon House at 8 o'clock. Booth said he himself should murder Mr. Lincoln and General Grant, Payne should take Mr. Seward and I should take Mr. Johnson. I told him I would not do it; that I had gone into the thing to capture, but I was not going to kill. He told me I was a fool; that I would be hung anyhow, and that it was death for every man that backed out; and so we parted. I wandered about the streets until about two o'clock and then went to the Kimmel House and from there pawned my pistol at Georgetown and went to my cousin's house in Montgomery County, where I was arrested the nineteenth following.

GEORGE ATZERODT.

It was a plan to carry off Lincoln and give him up to the Confederates, but when that failed, Booth proposed to kill Lincoln and all the Cabinet. All the rest backed out and scattered like a lot of beggars. We never heard of Surratt, or Arnold or any of them again. I told Booth that I would go with him, and he preferred to kill Lincoln, while I was set upon Seward. I deserve to be killed and so does Booth. The rest were women and babies.

LEWIS PAYNE.

LIBRARY OF CONGRESS

Howard's Livery Stable

I carry bills for Ford's Theatre during the daytime, and stand at the stage-door at night. I knew John Wilkes Booth and used to attend his horse, and see that it was fed and cleaned. His stable was immediately back of the theater. Between 9 and 10 o'clock that night, I heard Deboney calling to Ned that Booth wanted him out in the alley. Spangler called me out there to hold it; so I held the horse.

JOSEPH BURROUGHS,
"Peanut John."

I keep the restaurant adjoining Ford's on the lower side. Booth came into my restaurant, I judge a little after 10 o'clock, walked up to the bar, and called for some whisky, which I gave him; he then called for some water, which I also gave him; he placed the money on the counter and went out. PETER TALTAVUL.

He was naturally a nervous man and restless in his movements. I remember he first came in and said as he took hold of two fingers, "What time of night is it?" I told him to step into the lobby and there he could see the clock. Next, he came and asked me to give him a chew of tobacco, which I readily did. Afterwards I went

NATIONAL PARK SERVICE

Kirkwood House, Where Atzerodt Was to Kill Vice-President Johnson

FRANK LESLIE'S ILLUSTRATED NEWSPAPER, MAY 13, 1865

Awaiting Booth's Last Exit

into the saloon just below the theater to get a drink, and Booth was there drinking. I went back to the door and he soon came again. He passed into the house and stood a moment looking at the audience, and then went out again. Shortly afterwards he returned and passed in and around upstairs into the balcony, humming a tune.

J. E. BUCKINGHAM, SR.,
doorkeeper.

Here we have five human beings in a narrow space—the greatest man of his time in the glory of the most stupendous success in our history, the idolized chief of a nation already mighty, with illimitable vistas of grandeur to come; his beloved wife, proud and happy; a pair of bethrothed lovers with all the promise of felicity that youth, wealth, social position could give them; and this young actor, handsome as Endymion on Latmos, the pet of his world. The glitter of fame, happiness and ease was upon the entire group, but in an instant everything was changed with the blinding swiftness of enchantment.

Quick death was to come to the central figure of that company, the central figure, we believe, of the great and good men of the century. Over all the rest the blackest fates lowered menacingly, fates from which a mother might pray that kindly death would save her children in infamy. One was to wander with the stain of murder on his soul, with the curses of a world upon his name, with a price set upon his head, in frightful physical pain till he died a dog's death in a burning barn; the stricken wife was to pass the rest of her days in melancholy and madness; of these two young lovers, one was to slay the other and then end his days a raving maniac.

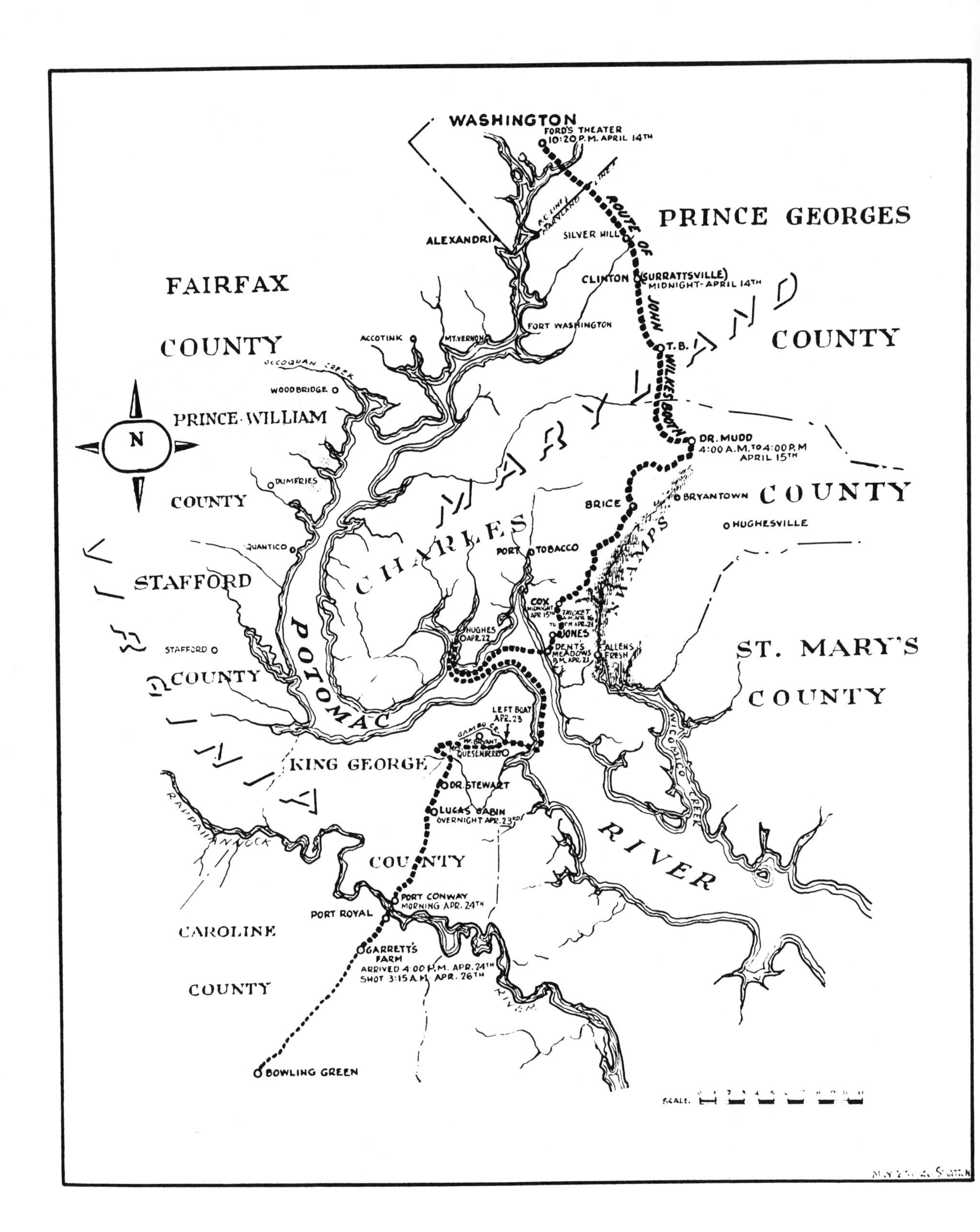
WASHINGTON
FORD'S THEATER
10:20 P.M. APRIL 14TH
ROUTE OF JOHN WILKES BOOTH
PRINCE GEORGES
ALEXANDRIA
SILVER HILL
CLINTON (SURRATTSVILLE)
MIDNIGHT-APRIL 14TH
FAIRFAX
COUNTY
ACCOTINK
MT. VERNON
FORT WASHINGTON
T.B.
COUNTY
OCCOQUAN CREEK
WOODBRIDGE
PRINCE-WILLIAM
COUNTY
N
DR. MUDD
4:00 A.M. TO 4:00 P.M
APRIL 15TH
DUMFRIES
BRICE
BRYANTOWN
COUNTY
HUGHESVILLE
CHARLES
QUANTICO
PORT TOBACCO
STAFFORD
COX
MIDNIGHT
APR 15TH
THICKET
JONES
DENTS
MEADOWS
P.M. APR. 21
ALLENS
FRESH
HUGHES
APR. 22
STAFFORD
COUNTY
POTOMAC
ST. MARY'S
COUNTY
LEFT BOAT
APR. 23
GAMBO CR.
MR. BRYANT
MR. QUESENBERRY
KING GEORGE
DR. STEWART
LUCAS CABIN
OVERNIGHT APR. 23RD
RAPPAHANNOCK
COUNTY
RIVER
WICOMICO CREEK
PORT CONWAY
MORNING APR. 24TH
PORT ROYAL
CAROLINE
COUNTY
GARRETT'S
FARM
ARRIVED 4:00 P.M. APR. 24TH
SHOT 3:15 A.M. APR. 26TH
BOWLING GREEN
SCALE

CHAPTER VII

FLIGHT INTO DARKNESS

ESCAPE

The Escape Route
NATIONAL PARK SERVICE

Beginning of the Flight FRANK LESLIE'S ILLUSTRATED NEWSPAPER, MAY 13, 1865

I was sitting in the front seat of the orchestra. The sharp report of a pistol startled me and simultaneously a man leaped from the President's box. At the same instant I jumped on the stage and the man disappeared at the lefthand stage entrance. I ran across the stage following calling out, "Stop that man!" three times. On opening the door I heard the tramping of a horse, the horse's feet rattling violently. I ran in the direction where the horse was heading. He brought the horse forward and spurred him, crouched forward down over the saddle, and soon swept rapidly toward F Street. JOSEPH B. STEWART.

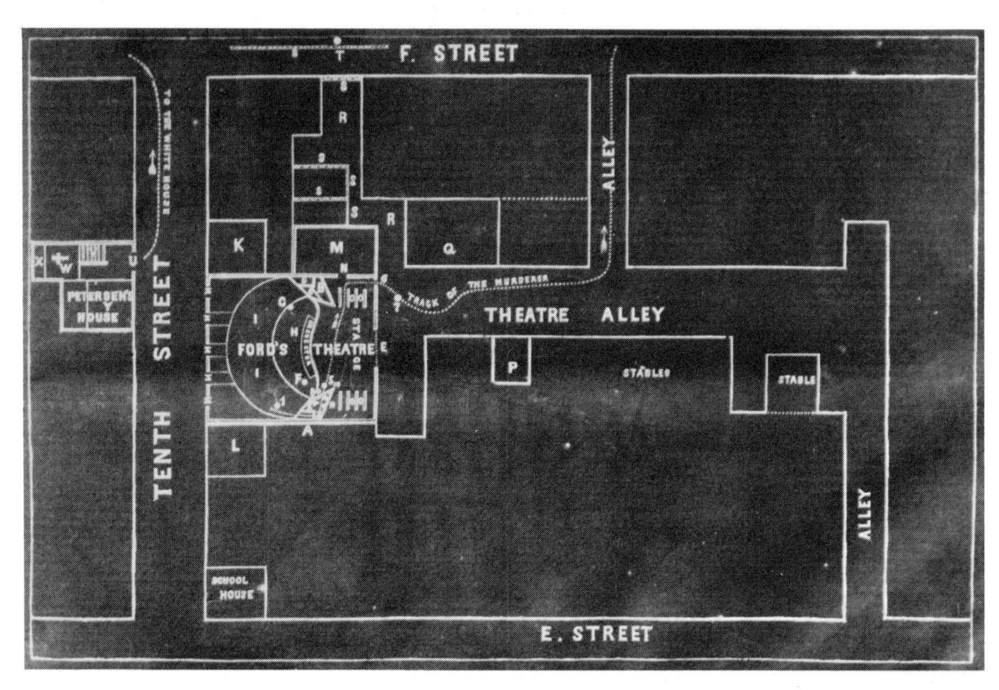

Nearby Streets and Alleys NATIONAL PARK SERVICE

On the night of the 14th of April, I was on duty at the Navy Yard bridge. At about half-past 10 or 11 o'clock, a man approached rapidly on horseback. The sentry challenged him, and I advanced to see if he was a proper person to pass.

I asked him, "Who are you, sir?" He said, "My name is Booth." I asked him where he was from. He made answer, "From the city." "Where are you going?" I said; and he replied, "I am going home." I asked him where his home was. He said it was in Charles. I asked him what town. He said he did not live in any town. I said, "You must live in some town." Said he, "I live close to Beantown; but do not live in the town." I asked him why he was out so late; if he did not know the rule that persons were not allowed to pass after 9 o'clock. He said it was new to him; that he had had somewhere to go in the city, and it was a dark night, and he thought he would have the moon to ride home by. I thought he was a proper person to pass and I passed him.

He rode a small-sized horse, and it looked as though he had just had a short burst —a short push, and seemed restive and uneasy, much more so than the rider. In all, I had some three or four minutes' conversation with him.

In perhaps five or ten minutes, another person came along. He did not seem to be riding so rapidly as the first, or his horse did not show signs of it as much as the first. I asked who he was, and he said that his name was Smith, and that he was going home; that he lived at the White Plains. I asked him how it was that he was out so late. He made use of a rather indelicate expression, and said that he had been in bad company. I brought him up before the guard-house door, so that the light shone full in his face and on his horse. After his explanation I allowed him to pass.

SERGEANT SILAS T. COBB.

LIBRARY OF CONGRESS

Navy Yard Bridge

On the night of the 14th of April last, I was on the Bryantown road, coming to Washington, and about 11 o'clock, when on Good Hope Hill, I met two horsemen, one about half a mile behind the other, and both riding very fast. The first asked me if a horseman had passed ahead. As the second horseman rode up, a lot of teamsters were passing at the time, and I heard him ask whether a horseman had passed ahead. I met the first horseman two miles and a half or three miles from the city, half-way up the hill. It was not over five or ten minutes before the second horseman came along. Both of them were riding very fast.

POLK GARDINER.

I reside at Mrs. Surratt's tavern, Surrattsville, and am engaged in hotel-keeping and farming. Just about midnight on Friday, Herold came into the house and said, "Lloyd, for God's sake, make haste and get those things." I did not make any reply, but went straight and got the carbines, supposing they were the parties Mrs. Surratt had referred to, though she didn't mention any names. Mrs. Surratt told me to give the carbines, whisky, and field-glass. I did not give them the rope and monkey-wrench.

Booth didn't come in. I did not know him. He remained on his horse. Herold came into the house and got a bottle of whisky, and took it out to him, and he drank while sitting on his horse. I do not think they remained over five minutes. They only took one of the carbines. Booth said he could not take his, because his leg was broken.

Just as they were about leaving, the man who was with Herold said, "I will tell you some news, if you want to hear it," or something to that effect. "Well," said he, "I am pretty certain that we have assassinated the President and Secretary Seward." The moon was shining when the men came, and they rode off at a pretty rapid gait. I was right smart in liquor that afternoon, and after night I got more so.

JOHN M. LLOYD.

Surratt Tavern

NATIONAL PARK SERVICE

Dr. Samuel A. Mudd

NATIONAL PARK SERVICE

On opening the door I found two men. One on a horse led by the other man who had tied his horse to a tree nearby. I aided the man in getting off his horse and into the house, and laid him on the sofa in my parlor. After getting a light I assisted him in getting upstairs where there were two beds, one of which he took. He seemed to be very much injured in the back, and complained very much of it. I did not see his face at all. He seemed to be tremulous and not inclined to talk, and had his cloak thrown around his head, and seemed inclined to sleep, as I thought, in order to ease himself; and every now and then he would groan pretty heavily. I then took a piece of the bandbox and split it in half, doubled it at right angles and took some paste and pasted it into a splint. On examination I found there was a straight fracture of the tibia about two inches above the ankle.

He continued still to suffer and complained of severe pain in the back especially when being moved. I have been shown the photograph of J. Wilkes Booth and I should not think that this was the man from any resemblance to the photograph; but from other causes I have every reason to believe he is the man whose leg I dressed.

I had occasion to cut his boot longitudinally, in front of the instep. It seems that when he left my house this boot was left behind.

After setting the wounded man's leg the best I could for the time, I think I walked around to my farm-yard, and when I returned breakfast was ready, and as this young man was up and knocking about, I asked him to come to breakfast. He did so, but the other man remained upstairs in bed. I have seen the photograph of Herold but I do not recognize it as that of this young man. He seemed to be well acquainted

Dr. Mudd's Residence NATIONAL PARK SERVICE

throughout the whole country and I asked his name. He gave it as Henston, and that of the wounded man as Tyser or Tyson.

The only thing that excited my suspicion, upon reflecting upon these circumstances, was that after breakfast, when I was about to leave for my farm-work, this young man asked me if I had a razor, that his friend desired to take a shave, as perhaps he would feel better. I had noticed that the wounded man had whiskers and a moustache when he came into the house. After dinner I went to see the patient and although he kept his face partly turned away from me, I noticed that he had lost his moustaches but still retained his whiskers. This young man asked me if I could fix up, clumsily, some crutches for his friend to hobble along with, and I went down to the old Englishman I had there, who had a saw and augur, and he and I made a rude pair of crutches out of a piece of plank and sent them to him.

After dinner this young man and I rode over to my father's place to see if we could get a carriage for the wounded man; but I found that the carriages were all out of repair except one, and we could not get that one. He then concluded to go to Bryantown for a conveyance to get his friend over as far as his friend Mr. Wilmer.

I judge that between four and five o'clock on Saturday afternoon they left my house. I do not know where they went. DR. SAMUEL A. MUDD.

I met two men on Sat. night, 15 April—about 9 o'clock. I had heard of the murder of the President. These men asked me the way to Mr. Burtle's in the dark, I could not see their faces. They told me to get my horse and show them the way. Before I got to Burtle's they asked me if I could take them to Capt. Cox. One was a small man. The other was lame and had a crutch.

When they got to Cox's they got off. It was near midnight. Cox came out with a candle. He said, "How do you do." They went in and remained 3 or 4 hours. I remained outside. When they came out they were alone. Cox did not come out with them. The small man went some little distance when the lame one said, "Don't you know I can't get on." The small man then came back and helped. The small man told me to put my hand under his fork and lift him up, which I did.

Before I got to Cox's, the small man said, "Don't you say anything. If you tell that you saw anybody, you will not live long." I saw nothing more of them. I got back home, which is 12 miles from Cox's, about sunrise. In all they paid me $12.00.

OSWALD SWANN.

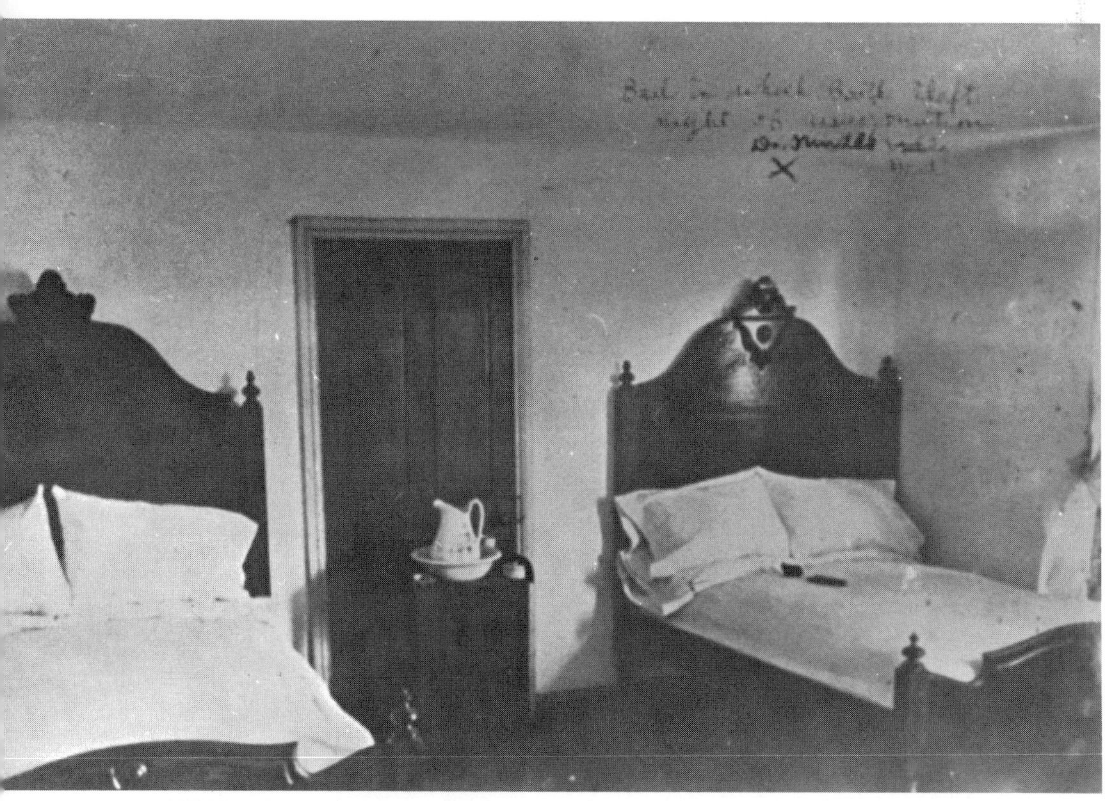

COURTESY DR. RICHARD D. MUDD

Guestroom Where Booth Slept

Thomas A. Jones

NATIONAL PARK SERVICE

The next morning, which was Easter Sunday, soon after breakfast, Samuel Cox, Jr., adopted son of my foster brother, Samuel Cox, came to my house, Huckleberry, and told me his father wanted to see me. He added, in an undertone, "Some strangers were at our house last night." It was a little after nine when we reached Rich Hill. Cox met me at the gate. At length, he said to me: "Tom, I had visitors about four o'clock this morning. They want to get across the river," and then added in a whisper, "Have you heard Lincoln was killed Friday night? Tom, we must get those men across the river."

He went on to say that about four that morning he was disturbed by a knock at the door. Upon opening the door he found a strange man standing there, while waiting at the gate was another stranger on horseback accompanied by a negro man of the neighborhood, named Oswald Swann. He went out to the man on horseback, who took him a little apart, out of the hearing of the negro, and told him what he had done. He showed him in India ink upon his wrist the initials J.W.B. He threw himself upon his mercy.

In the cause of the Confederacy I was willing to risk my life as I had often done. But the war was over. I knew that the whole of southern Maryland would soon be swarming with soldiers and detectives, eager to apprehend the murderer and reap the reward. "Sam," I replied, "I will see what I can do, but the odds are against me. I must see these men." He had sent them to a place in a piece of pine about one mile to the west of his house. The place was about two hundred yards south of the present village of Cox Station.

I stopped and gave the whistle. Presently a young man—he looked scarcely more than a boy—came cautiously out of the thicket. He carried a carbine ready cocked in his hands.

"I come from Cox, he told me I would find you here. I am a friend; you have nothing to fear from me." He said, "Follow me," and led the way for about thirty yards into the thick undergrowth to where his companion was lying. "This friend comes from Captain Cox," he said; and that was my introduction to John Wilkes Booth.

He was lying on the ground with his head supported on his hand. His carbine, pistols and knife were close beside him. A blanket was drawn partly over him. His slouch hat and crutch were lying by him. He was exceedingly pale and his features bore the evident traces of suffering. I have seldom seen a more strikingly handsome man.

THOMAS A. JONES.

Until today nothing was ever thought of sacrificing to our country's wrongs. For six months we have worked to capture. But our cause being almost lost, something decisive and great must be done. But its failure was owing to others who did not strike for their country with a heart. I struck boldly, and not as the papers say. I walked with a firm step through a thousand of his friends; was stopped but pushed on. A colonel was at his side. I shouted Sic semper before I fired. In jumping I broke my leg. I passed all his pickets. Rode sixty miles that night, with the bone of my leg tearing the flesh at every jump.

I can never repent it, though we hated to kill. Our country owed all our troubles to him, and God simply made me the instrument of his punishment.

The country is not what it was. This forced union is not what I have loved. I care not what becomes of me. I have no desire to outlive my country. This night (before the deed) I wrote a long article and left it for one of the editors of the *National Intelligencer,* in which I fully set forth our reasons for our proceedings. He or the Gov't. . . .

FROM BOOTH'S DIARY.

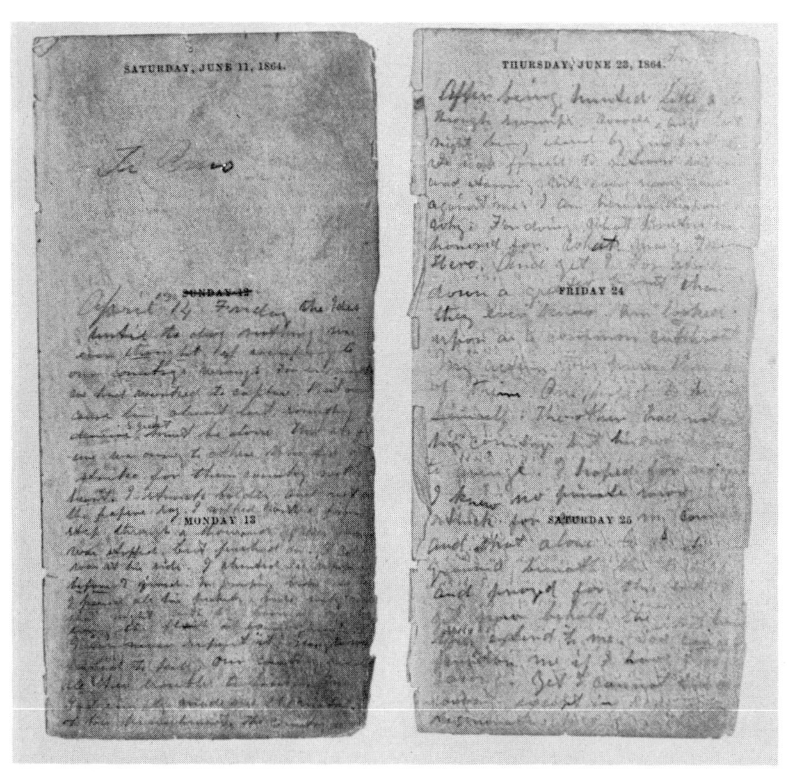
SATURDAY, JUNE 11, 1864.

SUNDAY 12

MONDAY 13

THURSDAY, JUNE 23, 1864.

FRIDAY 24

SATURDAY 25

NATIONAL PARK SERVICE

Booth's Diary

Huckleberry, the Home of Tom Jones NATIONAL PARK SERVICE

No sooner had I seen him in his helpless and suffering condition than I gave my whole mind to the problem of how to get him across the river. I told him that for the present he must remain where he was. I promised to bring him food every day, and to get him across the river just as soon as it would not be suicidal to make the attempt.

He said he knew the Government would use every means in its power to secure his capture. "But," he added, with a flash of determination lighting up his dark eye, "John Wilkes Booth will never be taken alive." He seemed very desirous to know what the world thought of his deed, and asked me to bring him some newspapers. Then promising to see them next day and bring food and newspapers, I mounted my horse and rode home.

After breakfast on Monday morning, I wrapped up some bread and butter and ham, filled a flask with coffee, and mounting my horse, set out on my dangerous visit to the daring assassin.

My plans were simply to keep myself informed as to what was going on and the first night the neighborhood was clear of soldiers and detectives to get my charges to the river. As the days rolled away, Booth's impatience to cross the river became almost insufferable. His leg, from neglect and exposure, had become terribly swollen and inflamed, and the pain he had to bear was excruciating. To add to his further discomfiture—if that was possible—a cold, cloudy, damp, spell of weather, such as we often have in spring, set in.

So through six long, wearisome days, and five dark and restless nights, Booth lay there in hiding. The only breaks in the monotony of that week were my daily visits, and the food and newspapers I carried him. He never tired of the newspapers. And there he read the world's just condemnation of his deed and the price that was offered for his life.

On Friday evening, one week after the assassination, I rode down to Allen's Fresh. A body of cavalry guided by John Walton rode in. Some of the soldiers entered Cotton's store, where I was sitting. Soon afterward Walton came in and exclaimed,

"Boys, I have news that they have been seen in St. Mary's," whereupon they all hastily remounted and galloped off. I left and as soon as I was out of the village I put whip to my horse and rode rapidly. It was dark by the time I reached the place. "The coast seems to be clear and darkness favors. Let us make the attempt," I said.

With difficulty Booth was raised by Herold and myself and placed upon my horse. Every movement, in spite of his stoicism, wrung a groan of anguish from his lips. The route we had to take was down the cart track, to the public road, a distance of about one mile and a half, then down the public road for another mile to the corner of my farm; and then through my place to the river, about one mile further, making the whole distance about three and a half miles. The night had grown inky dark.

At last we reached my place. We stopped under a pear tree near the stable. It was between nine and ten o'clock. "Wait here," I said, "while I go in and get you some supper, which you can eat while I get something for myself." "Oh," said Booth, "can't I go in and get some of your hot coffee?" It cut me to the heart when this poor creature made this piteous request to be allowed to enter a human habitation. I answered, "My friend, it wouldn't do. Indeed it would not be safe. Remember this is your last chance to get away."

I selected what I thought was enough for two men and carried it out to them. After supper we resumed our journey across the open field toward the longed-for river. Presently we came to a fence across the path, so we left the horse there and Herold and myself assisted Booth to dismount. The path was steep and narrow for three men to walk abreast.

At last we reached the shore and found the boat. It was a flat-bottomed boat about twelve feet long, of dark lead color. I had bought it in Baltimore the year before. We placed Booth in the stern with an oar to steer; Herold took the bow seat to row. Then lighting a candle which I had brought along for the purpose and carefully shading it with an oilcloth coat, I pointed out on the compass Booth had with him the course to steer.

"Keep to that," I said, "and it will bring you into Machodoc Creek. Mrs. Quesenberry lives near the mouth of that creek. If you tell her you come from me I think she will take care of you." As I was in the act of shoving the boat off Booth exclaimed, "Wait a minute, old fellow." He then offered me some money. I took eighteen dollars, the price of the boat I knew I would never see again. He wanted me to take more, but I said no, what I had done was not for money. He said, "God bless you, my dear friend, for all you have done. Good bye, old fellow." I pushed the boat off and it glided out of sight into the darkness.

THOMAS A. JONES.

FROM BAKER'S HISTORY OF THE U.S. SECRET SERVICE *Crossing the Potomac*

The Compass
NATIONAL PARK SERVICE

Friday, 21.—After being hunted like a dog through swamps and woods, and last night being chased by gun boats till I was forced to return, wet, cold, and starving, with every man's hand against me, I am here in despair. And why? For doing what Brutus was honored for, what made William Tell a Hero. And yet I for striking down an even greater tyrant than they ever knew, am looked upon as a common cutthroat. My act was purer than either of theirs. One hoped to be great himself. The other had not only his country's, but his own, wrongs to avenge. I hoped for no gain; I knew no private wrong. I struck for my country, and her alone. A people ground beneath this tyranny prayed for this end, and yet now see the cold hands they extend to me. God cannot pardon me if I have done wrong; yet I cannot see any wrong, except in serving a degenerate people. The little, the very little, I left behind to clear my name, the Government will not allow to be printed. So ends all. For my country I have given up all that makes life sweet and Holy, brought misery upon my family, and am sure there is no pardon for me in the heavens, since man condemns me so. I have only *heard* of what has been done (except what I did myself), and it fills me with horror. God, try and forgive me and bless my mother. To-night I will once more try the river, with the intent to cross, though I have a greater desire and almost a mind to return to Washington, and in a measure clear my name, which I feel I can do.

I do not repent the blow I struck. I may before my God, but not to man. I think I have done well, though I am abandoned, with the curse of Cain upon me, when, if the world knew my heart, that *one blow* would have made me great, though I did desire no greatness. To-night I try to escape these bloodhounds once more. Who, who, can read his fate? God's will be done. I have too great a soul to die like a criminal. Oh! may He spare me that, and let me die bravely. I bless the entire world. Have never hated nor wronged any one. This last was not a wrong, unless God deems it so, and it is with Him to damn or bless me. And for this brave boy with me, who often prays (yes, before and since) with a true and sincere heart, was it a crime in him? If so, why can he pray the same? I do not wish to shed a drop of blood, but I must fight the course. 'Tis all that's left me. FROM BOOTH'S DIARY.

It is well known that Booth did not succeed in crossing the river that night. The strong flood-tide, against which I had forgotten to caution him, swept the boat up the river, and sometime during the night he and Herold landed at a place near Naugemoy stores, still in Maryland. They stayed hidden somewhere in the neighborhood during Saturday, and at night succeeded in crossing to Virginia, and reached

Mrs. Quesenberry's Sunday morning. Here they were met by my brother-in-law, Thomas H. Harbin, and a man named Joseph Badden, who did all they could to assist them, showed them a hiding place, carried them food from Mrs. Quesenberry's, and finally put them in charge of an old man named Boyan, who took them on to Dr. Richard Stewart.

THOMAS A. JONES.

Two men were brought to my house on the night of Sunday, April 23. I was in bed and asleep. My dogs were barking and woke me up. I heard a horse and I thought there might be some one trying to steal my horses. A strange voice called me. I would not open the door, but asked who it was. I was frightened at the time. People had been shot in that way, and I was afraid to come out.

One of the men said, "We want to stay here tonight." I said, "You cannot do it; I am a colored man and have no right to take care of white people; I have only one room in the house, and my wife is sick." He said, "We are Confederate soldiers; we have been in service 3 years; we have been knocking about all night, and don't intend to any longer; but we are going to stay."

By that time the one with crutches had got into the house. I said, "Gentlemen, you have treated me very badly." The lame man was sitting down then, and he reached behind me, took out a bowie knife, and flourished it, saying, "Old man, how do you like that." He said, "We were sent here, old man; we understand you have good teams." He said to the other, "Well, Dave, we will stay here, and make this old man get us this horse in the morning."

I was afraid to go to sleep, and my wife and I went out on the step and stayed there the rest of the night. In the morning they asked me what I got for driving to Port Conway. I said $10 in gold or $20 in green-backs. My son, 20 or 21 years old, drove the team. My house is about ten miles from Port Conway, and 3 miles from the Potomac. They started away about 7 o'clock, I think in the morning of Monday, April 24th.

WILLIAM LUCAS.

NATIONAL PARK SERVICE

The Lucas Cabin

I was on my way from Fauquier County (where I had been with Mosby's command) to Caroline County, Virginia, in company with Lieutenant Ruggles and a young man named Bainbridge. At Port Conway, on the Rappahannock, I saw a wagon down on the wharf, at the ferry, on the Monday week after the assassination of President Lincoln. A young man got out of it, came toward us, and asked us what command we belonged to. We were all dressed in Confederate uniform. Lieutenant Ruggles said, "We belong to Mosby's command."

He then said, "If I am not inquisitive, can I ask where you are going?" I spoke, then, and replied, "That's a secret, where we are going." After this we went back on the wharf, and a man with crutches got out of the wagon. One of us asked him what command he belonged to, and he replied, "To A.P. Hill's corps." Herold told us their name was Boyd; that his brother was wounded below Petersburg, and asked if we would take him out of the lines.

After we had talked a very short time, Herold touched me on the shoulder and said he wanted to speak to me; he carried me down to the wharf, and said, "I suppose you are raising a command to go South?" and added that he would like to go along with us. At length I said, "I can not go with any man that I don't know anything about." He seemed very much agitated, and then remarked, "We are the assassinators of the President." I was so much confounded that I did not make any reply then that I remember. Lieutenant Ruggles was very near, watering his horse; I called to him, and he came there, and either Herold or myself remarked to Lieutenant Ruggles that they were the assassinators of the President. Booth then came up, and Herold introduced himself to us, and then introduced Booth. Herold passed himself off to us first as Boyd, and said he wanted to pass under that name. He afterward told us their true names were Herold and Booth, but they kept the name of Boyd. Booth, I remember, had on his hand "J.W.B."

Then we went across the river. Booth rode Ruggles's horse. Herold was walking. We then went on up to Mr. Garrett's, and there we left Booth. Herold and all of us went on up the road, then, to within a few miles of Bowling Green. Bainbridge and Herold went to Mrs. Clark's, and Ruggles and myself to Bowling Green. The next day Herold came to Bowling Green, spent the day, had dinner, and left in the evening, and that was the last I saw of him, except the night that they were caught.

WILLIE S. JETT.

Booth and Herold both seemed to be the worse for their exposure and hardships of the past few days. Booth wore a black soft hat, dark clothes, one cavalry boot, the one on his wounded leg having been cut off, and his weapons were a carbine, two revolvers, and a knife, the blade of the latter bearing the stain of blood, for with it he had wounded Major Rathbone. I noticed that his wounded leg was greatly swollen,

NATIONAL PARK SERVICE *Richard Garrett's House*

inflamed and dark, as from bruised blood, while it seemed to have been wretchedly dressed, the splints being simply pasteboard rudely tied about it. That he suffered intense pain all the time there was no doubt, though he tried to conceal his agony.

LIEUT. M.B. RUGGLES.

This man, whom I and all my family looked upon as Mr. Boyd, a wounded Confederate soldier, was taken at once into my house. He supped with my family, and slept that night in one of my upper rooms, in which my sons and two smaller children slept. He remained in the house and yard, most of the time reclining on the grass. He had very little to say and seemed to be suffering, we thought from his wound.

RICHARD GARRETT.

SURRAT.

BOOTH.

HAROLD.

War Department, Washington, April 20, 1865.

$100,000 REWARD!

THE MURDERER

Of our late beloved President, Abraham Lincoln,

IS STILL AT LARGE.

$50,000 REWARD

Will be paid by this Department for his apprehension, in addition to any reward offered by Municipal Authorities or State Executives.

$25,000 REWARD

Will be paid for the apprehension of JOHN H. SURRAT, one of Booth's Accomplices.

$25,000 REWARD

Will be paid for the apprehension of David C. Harold, another of Booth's accomplices.

LIBERAL REWARDS will be paid for any information that shall conduce to the arrest of either of the above-named criminals, or their accomplices.

All persons harboring or secreting the said persons, or either of them, or aiding or assisting their concealment or escape, will be treated as accomplices in the murder of the President and the attempted assassination of the Secretary of State, and shall be subject to trial before a Military Commission and the punishment of DEATH.

Let the stain of innocent blood be removed from the land by the arrest and pu[illegible]urderers.

All good citizens are exhorted to aid public justice on this occasion. Every man should consider his own conscience charged with this solemn duty, and rest neither night nor day until it be accomplished.

EDWIN M. STANTON, Secretary of War.

DESCRIPTIONS.—BOOTH is Five Feet 7 or 8 inches high, slender build, high forehead, black hair, black eyes, and wore a heavy black moustache, which there is some reason to believe has been shaved off.

JOHN H. SURRAT is about 5 feet, 9 inches. Hair rather thin and dark; eyes rather light; no beard. Would weigh 145 or 150 pounds. Complexion rather pale and clear, with color in his cheeks. Wore light clothes of fine quality. Shoulders square; cheek bones rather prominent; chin narrow; ears projecting at the top; forehead rather low and square, but broad. Parts his hair on the right side; neck rather long. His lips are firmly set. A slim man.

DAVID C. HAROLD is five feet six inches high, hair dark, eyes dark, eyebrows rather heavy, full face, nose short, haud short and fleshy, feet small, instep high, round bodied, naturally quick and active, slightly closes his eyes when looking at a person.

NOTICE.—In addition to the above, State and other authorities have offered rewards amounting to almost one hundred thousand dollars, making an aggregate of about **TWO HUNDRED THOUSAND DOLLARS.**

CHAPTER VIII

ONE-HUNDRED-THOUSAND-DOLLAR REWARD

PURSUIT AND CAPTURE

Colonel Lafayette C. Baker NATIONAL ARCHIVES

At twelve o'clock Saturday, April 15, I received the following dispatch:—

Colonel L. C. Baker:—

Come here immediately and see if you can find the murderer of the President.

EDWIN M. STANTON,
Secretary of War.

As I entered the Secretary's office, he turned away to hide his tears. He remarked—"Well, Baker, they have now performed what they have long threatened to do. You must go to work. My whole dependence is upon you."

A good many soldiers came there on Saturday, and on Sunday night others came. When they asked me if I had seen two men pass that way in the morning, I told them I had not.

JOHN M. LLOYD,
tavern keeper.

Saturday evening, just about the time Booth and Herold were setting out from Dr. Mudd's, I was near Pope's Creek, when two Federal soldiers asked me whose boat that was down in the creek, I told them it was mine. "Well," one of them replied, "you had better keep an eye on it. There are suspicious characters in the neighborhood who will be wanting to cross the river. Our President was assassinated last night."

On Monday morning while we were talking I heard the clanking of sabres and trampling of horses, as a body of cavalry passed down the road within two hundred yards of us. We listened with suspended breath until the sound died away in the distance. I then said, "You see, my friends, we must wait." "Yes," he (Booth) answered, "I leave it all to you." There were but two boats on this side of the river that I knew of, and they were both mine. Why the government did not take possession at once has always been a mystery to me. The neighborhood was full with cavalrymen and detectives. They visited my house several times during that week (as they did every house in southern Maryland) and upon one occasion searched it.

Tuesday morning I rode up to Port Tobacco. In Port Tobacco I made the acquaintance of Captain Williams. He was standing in the bar-room of the old Brawner Hotel in the act of drinking with several gentlemen, when I entered. He politely invited me to drink with him. Just as we were about to take the drink, he turned to me and said, "I will give one hundred thousand dollars to any one who will give me the information that will lead to Booth's capture." I replied, "That is a large sum of money and ought to get him if money can do it."

THOMAS A. JONES.

NATIONAL PARK SERVICE

Brawner Hotel, Port Tobacco

The Arrest of Payne at the Surratt House

NATIONAL PARK SERVICE

About twenty minutes past 11 o'clock, on the evening of the 17th of April, Colonel Olcott gave me instructions to go to the house of Mrs. Surratt, 541 H Street, and superintend the seizing of papers, and the arrest of the inmates of the house. I arrived there about half-past 11 o'clock, and found Major Smith, Captain Wermerskirch, and some other officers, who had been there about ten minutes. The inmates were in the parlor, about ready to leave.

I heard a knock and a ring at the door. At the same time Captain Wermerskirch and myself stepped forward and opened the door, when the prisoner, Payne, came in with a pickaxe over his shoulder, dressed in a gray coat, gray vest, black pants, and a hat made out of, I should judge, the sleeve of a shirt or the leg of a drawer. Said he, "I guess I am mistaken." Said I, "Whom do you want to see?" "Mrs. Surratt," said he. I asked him what he came there at this time of night for. He said he came to dig a gutter; Mrs. Surratt had sent for him. I asked him when. He said, "In the morning." I asked him why he came at this time of night to go to work. He said he simply called to find out what time he should go to work in the morning. I asked him if he had any previous acquaintance with Mrs. Surratt. He said, "No." Then I asked him why she selected him. He said she knew he was working around the neighborhood, and was a

The Pickaxe
NATIONAL PARK SERVICE

poor man, and came to him. I asked him how old he was. He said, "About twenty." Previous to this he pulled out an oath of allegiance, and on the oath of allegiance was, "Lewis Payne, Fauquier County, Virginia." That is the pickaxe he had on his shoulder.
R. C. MORGAN.

Major Smith asked Mrs. Surratt whether she knew him, and Mrs. Surratt, in the presence of Payne, held up one or both her hands, and said, "Before God, I have never seen that man before. I have not hired him; I do not know any thing about him"; or words to that effect.
CAPTAIN W. M. WERMERSKIRCH.

An Incriminating Picture
I found this in the back room of the first floor of Mrs. Surratt's house. The back part was all sealed, my curiosity was excited by noticing a piece torn off the back. I opened the back and found the likeness of J. Wilkes Booth.

NATIONAL PARK SERVICE

The Boot

On Friday, the 21st of April, I went to Dr. Mudd's again for the purpose of arresting him. When he found we were going to search the house he said something to his wife, and she went upstairs and brought down a boot. Mudd said he had cut it off the man's leg. I turned down the top of the boot and saw the name "J. Wilkes" written in it.

NATIONAL PARK SERVICE

I was set about procuring photographs, not only of Booth and Herold, but the entire Confederate cabinet as well, for it was suspected of having instigated the whole murderous business. With a half dozen men I was sent into lower Maryland to scatter all over these pictures and descriptions, together with flaming handbills advertising large rewards, and if possible gain some clues as to the direction the fugitives had taken. We returned to Washington, having accomplished nothing, and all this time the men we wanted were hiding in the swamps of that very locality.

The large reward offered ($100,000) filled the whole country between Washington and Port Tobacco with detectives. They would not work with us or give us any information. They preferred rather to throw us off the trail. And so over ten days had gone by and the murderers were still at large.

But now one of our detectives was ordered to take with him a telegraph operator with instruments and go into lower Maryland, and act as a medium of communication with the capital. There men answering the description of Booth and Herold had crossed the Potomac the Saturday night before. It was believed the trail was found. An order was sent for twenty-five men to serve as escort.

A half hour later Lt. Doherty of the 16th New York Cavalry had reported to Gen. Baker for orders and was directed by him to go with us. Conger and I mounted and ordered the guard to follow and soon all were aboard the government tug "John S. Ide," and were steaming down the Potomac. At ten in the evening we were at Belle Plain landing. Our chief had advised us to leave the tug at this landing, take our horses and scour the country. At daylight (Tuesday) we decided to strike across the country in the direction of Port Conway, a little town on the Rappahannock, southwesterly from Belle Plain.

Lieut. E. P. Doherty

The parties who made the arrest of Booth and Herold were a detachment of the 16th New York Cavalry, consisting of Lt. E. P. Doherty, commanding, two sergeants, seven corporals and seventeen privates; accompanied by E. J. Conger and L. B. Baker, two employees in the detective service of Col. L. C. Baker. Report of Generals Holt and Townsend.

NATIONAL PARK SERVICE

COURTESY MAURICE J. BAKER

Lieut. Luther B. Baker, Col. L. C. Baker, Col. E. J. Conger

Conger was nearly exhausted and lay down for a rest, as did also the command with the exception of one man whom I took with me to the ferry. I found a fisherman whose name was Rollins. I asked him if a lame man had crossed the river there with(in) a few days. "Yes," he replied, "and there was another man with him." I showed him my photographs. He at once pointed to the pictures of Booth and Herold and said, "These are the men, but this," referring to Booth, "had no mustache." I was the fortunate one among all the eager thousands in the search. My corporal was sent back to the farm-house for Conger and Dougherty to come with the command, to the ferry.

Then alone with the fisherman, I plied him with questions. "When did you see these men?" "Yesterday." "Where did they go?" "I do not know certainly," he said. "They had hired me to take them across the river, but two men came up who seemed to know them and they four went across the river together." "Who were these men who came up?" "One of them said he was Capt. Jett and the other Lieut. Bainbridge." "Do you know where they went?" "Well, this Capt. Jett has a ladylove over at Bowling Green and I reckon they might have gone there. Bowling Green is about fifteen miles south and west from here. It is a watering place, a big hotel there and not much of anything else. It would be a good place for a lame man to stay." I said, "You must go with us to Bowling Green and show us the way."

Conger came down to the ferry with the command. It was decided to follow this lead at once. Booth had managed to evade all pursuers, and crossed the Potomac and not less than forty miles of country between it and the Rappahannock, and had been taken across the river at this point only yesterday. The ferry-boat was hailed and it took us three trips.

It was nearly sundown. Booth was at that moment only a half a mile from us at Garrett's. We passed the place only a few moments later; but we believed him to be at Bowling Green fifteen miles away and we pushed on, leaving behind us the man we wanted so much to capture. LIEUT. LUTHER B. BAKER.

Captain Ruggles and I went on the next morning towards Port Royal, Herold accompanying us as far as Garrett's gate, where we left him. Just before reaching Port Royal I met a soldier who told me that if we did not want to be captured to turn back. Said he, "The town is full of Yankees in search of Booth, who, they say, crossed the river yesterday." We turned and rode back to Garrett's. I remember pointing to a thick piece of woodland, and saying, "Booth, get over there and hide yourself." He replied, "I'll do as you say. Rest assured of one thing, Wilkes Booth will never be taken alive." A. R. BAINBRIDGE.

On their return they learned that the troops had gone on toward Bowling Green. My father had become suspicious so after supper he told them they could not sleep in the house. Brother Jack and I went with them to the barn and after they entered, fearing they might take our horses, we locked the door. We concluded to sleep in a shuck house near by to guard our horses. WILLIAM GARRETT.

Monitor "Saugus"
The monitors "Montauk" and "Saugus" had been designated for service as a prison for the reception and safekeeping of the prisoners.

NATIONAL ARCHIVES

COURTESY CLAUDE SIMMONS

Goldman Inn, Bowling Green

I went into a room at a hotel at Bowling Green, and found these two men in bed. One began to get up. I said to him, "Is your name Jett?" He said, "Yes sir." Said I, "Get up; I want you."

On the night of the capture, I found Jett in bed in a hotel in Bowling Green. I told him that I wanted him. He put on his pants, and came out to me in the front part of the room. I said, "Where are the two men who came with you across the river?" He said, "They are on the road to Port Royal, about three miles this side of that." "At whose house are they?" I asked. "Mr. Garrett's," he replied; "I will go there with you and show you where they are now, and you can get them." I said to him, "You say they are on the road to Port Royal?" "Yes, sir." I said to him, "I have just come from there." Said he, "If you have come that way, you have come past them." We went back to Mr. Garrett's house. We rode rapidly up to the house and barn, and stationed the men around the house and quarters.

The first individual we saw was an old man, whose name was Garrett. I said to him, "Where are the two men who stopped here at your house?" "They have gone." He then commenced to tell me that they came there without his consent. I said to him, "I do not want any long story out of you; I just want to know where these men have gone." He commenced over again to tell me, and I said to one of the men, "Bring in a lariat rope here, and I will put that man up to the top of one of those locust trees." One of his sons then came in and said, "Don't hurt the old man; he is scared. I will tell you where the men are you want to find." Said I, "That is what I want to know; where are they?" He said, "In the barn."

We went to the barn, and stationed the remaining part of the men. I heard somebody walking around inside on the hay. By that time another Garrett had come from somewhere; and Lieutenant Baker said to one of them, "You must go in the barn and get the arms from those men." Baker said to the men inside, "We are going to send this man in to get your arms, and you must come out and deliver yourselves up." Garrett went in, and he came out very soon and said, "This man says 'Damn you, you have betrayed me,' and threatened to shoot me." I then directed Lieutenant Baker

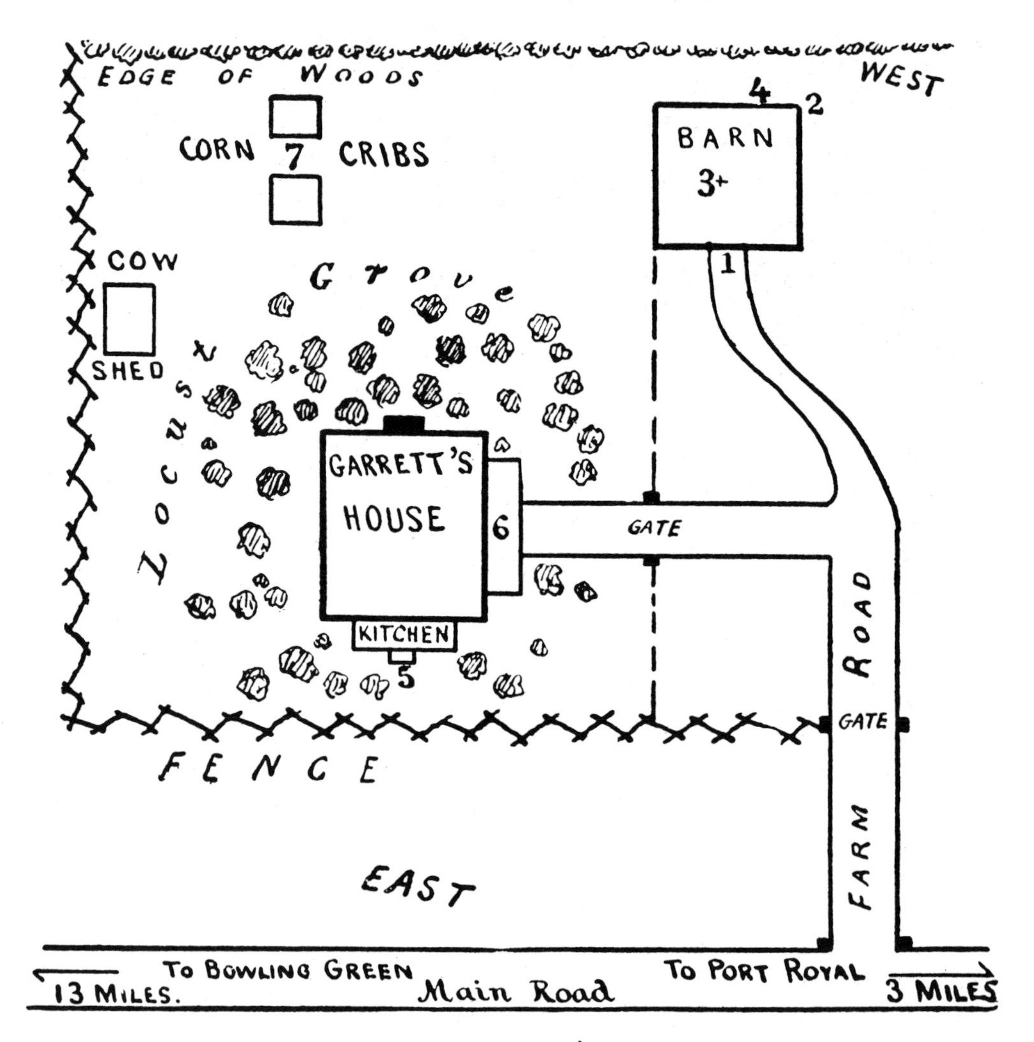

PLAN OF GARRETT'S PLACE.

1. Door of barn through which Booth was brought.
2. Corner of barn which was fired.
3. Where Booth stood.
4. Where Boston Corbett stood.
5. Door of kitchen of house where Baker met Garrett.
6. Front porch, on which Booth died.
7. Corn cribs, where the two Garrett boys slept.

Plan of Garrett's Place FROM OLDROYD'S ASSASSINATION OF ABRAHAM LINCOLN

to tell them that if they would come out and deliver themselves up, very well; if not, in five minutes we would set the barn on fire. Booth replied; "Who are you; what do you want; whom do you want?" Lieutenant Baker said, "We want you, and we know who you are; give up your arms and come out." He replied, "Let us have a little time to consider it." Lieutenant Baker said, "Very well"; and some ten or fifteen minutes probably intervened. He asked again, "Who are you, and what do you want?" The reply was made to him, "It don't make any difference who we are; we want to take you prisoners." Said he, "This is a hard case; it may be I am to be taken by my friends." Some time in the conversation he said, "Captain, I know you to be a brave man, and I believe you to be honorable; I am a cripple. I have got but one leg; If you will withdraw your men in 'line' one hundred yards from the door, I will come out and fight you." Lieutenant Baker replied that he did not want any fight with him. Once more after this he said, "If you'll take your men fifty yards from the door, I'll come out and fight you; give me a chance for my life." The same reply was made to him. His answer to that was in a singular theatrical voice, "Well, my brave boys, prepare a stretcher for me."

Some time passed before any further conversation was held with him. In the meantime I requested one of the Garretts to pile some brush up against the corner of the barn—pine boughs. After awhile Booth said, "There's a man in here wants to come out." Lieutenant Baker said "Very well, let him hand his arms out and come out." One of the expressions made use of by Booth to Herold, "You damned coward, will you leave now? Go, go; I would not have you stay with me." He came to the door and said, "Let me out." Lieutenant Baker said to him, "Hand out your arms." The reply was, "The arms are mine, and I have got them." Baker said, "This man carried a carbine, and he must hand it out." Booth said, "Upon the word and honor of a gentleman, he has no arms; the arms are mine, and I have got them." The door was opened, he stuck out his hands; Lieutenant Baker took hold of him, brought him out, and passed him to the rear. I went around to the corner of the barn, pulled some hay out, twisted up a little of it, set fire to it, and stuck it back through on top of the hay. It blazed very rapidly—lit right up at once.

I put my eye up to the crack next to the one the fire was put through, and looked in. The only thing I noticed he had in his hands was a carbine. He came back, and looked along the cracks one after another, rapidly. He looked at the fire. He dropped his arm, relaxed his muscles, turned around, and started for the door at the front of the barn. I ran around to the other side, and when about half round I heard the report of a pistol.

LIEUT. COL. EVERTON J. CONGER,
in charge of the pursuit.

Booth's Carbine

NATIONAL PARK SERVICE

HARPER'S WEEKLY, MAY 13, 1865

Fateful Decision

In an instant it was light inside. I peered in and could see Booth distinctly. He started forward as if to extinguish the fire. He now turned, dropped one crutch, and with the aid of the other came toward the door, drew himself up to his full height and seemed to take in the entire situation.

Booth's Probable Suicide Weapon

NATIONAL PARK SERVICE

After Herold was taken out, the detective, Mr. Conger, came round to the side of the barn where I was and set fire to the hay. I knew Booth could distinguish me through those cracks and could pick us off. I saw him make a movement toward the door. I supposed he was going to fight his way out. One of the men, who was watching him, told me that he aimed his carbine at me. My mind was upon him attentively to see that he did no harm, and when I became impressed that it was time I shot him I took steady aim on my arm, and shot him through a large crack in the barn. It was not through fear at all that I shot him, but because it was my impression that it was time the man was shot; for I thought he would do harm to our men in trying to fight his way through that den, if I did not. SERGEANT BOSTON CORBETT.

This Boston Corbett was a very eccentric character. He was not considered to be quite up to the normal standard in intellectual capacity, but was unique in his religious development. He would shout in a sharp, shrill voice, "Amen! Glory to God!" All remonstrance was in vain. Just as day was breaking, as he was crossing the lawn he was pointed out to Conger as the man who did the shooting. Conger hailed him with some profanity and demanded to know why he shot against orders. Corbett pointed heavenward and said, "Colonel, God Almighty directed me." "Well," said Conger, turning on his heel, "I guess He did or you couldn't have hit him through that crack in the barn." LIEUTENANT BAKER.

Boston Corbett
LIBRARY OF CONGRESS

I went right to the door, and went into the barn and found Lieutenant Baker looking at Booth, holding him, or raising him up, I do not know which. I said to him, "He shot himself." Said he, "No, he did not, either." Said I, "Whereabouts is he shot —in the head or neck?" I raised him then, and looked on the right side of the neck, and saw a place where the blood was running out. I said, "Yes, sir; he shot himself." Lieutenant Baker replied very earnestly that he did not. I then said, "Let us carry him out of here; this will soon be burning." We took him up and carried him out on the grass. I went back into the barn to see if the fire could be put down; it was burning so fast, and there was no water and nothing to help with. I then went back. Before this, I supposed him to be dead. He had all the appearance of a dead man; but when I got back to him, his eyes and mouth were moving. I called immediately for some water, and put it on his face, and he somewhat revived, and attempted to speak, and finally I understood him to say, "Tell mother I die for my country." They carried him from there to the porch of Mr. Garrett's house, and laid him on an old straw bed, or tick. By that time he revived considerably; he could then talk in a

Unceremonious Exit FRANK LESLIE'S ILLUSTRATED NEWSPAPER, MAY 13, 1865

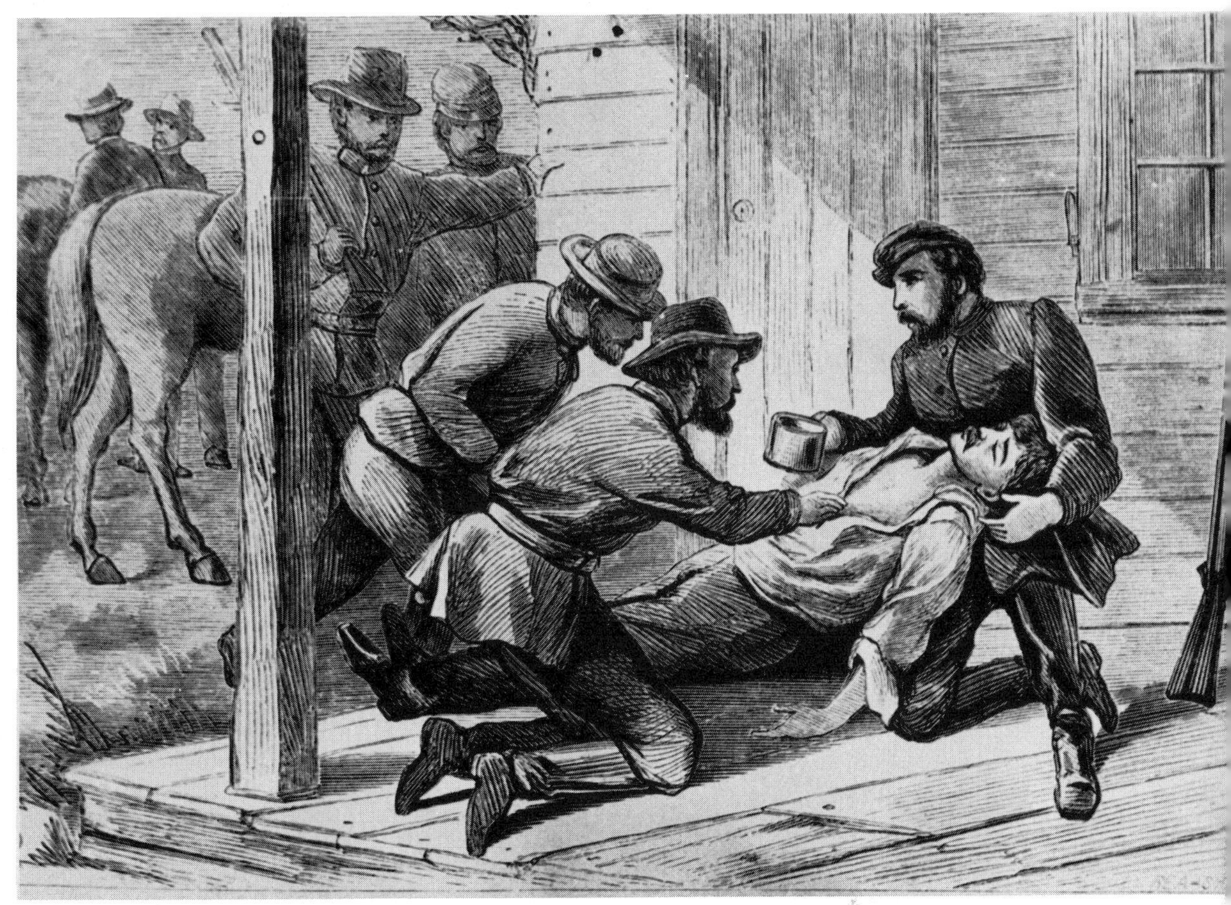

FROM BAKER'S HISTORY OF THE U.S. SECRET SERVICE

Last Moments

whisper. He wanted water; we gave it to him. He wanted to be turned on his face. I said to him, "You can not lie on your face"; and he wanted to be turned on his side; we turned him upon his side three times, I think, but he could not lie with any comfort, and wanted to be turned immediately back. He asked me to put my hand on his throat and press down, which I did, and he said, "Harder." I pressed down as hard as I thought necessary, and he made very strong exertions to cough, but was unable to do so—no muscular exertion could he make. I supposed he thought something was in his throat. He repeated two or three times, "Kill me, kill me." The reply was made to him, "We don't want to kill you; we want you to get well." I then took what things were in his pockets, and tied them up in a piece of paper. He was not then quite dead. He would—once, perhaps, in five minutes—gasp; his heart would almost die out, and then it would commence again, and by a few rapid beats would make a slight motion.

LIEUTENANT COLONEL CONGER.

Return of Booth and Herold NATIONAL PARK SERVICE

Conger had started for Washington, taking with him Booth's arms, diary and whatever else was upon his person. The body was quickly wrapped in a blanket that had been folded and used as a saddle cloth and sewed together. Then it was placed in an old market wagon, with an aged colored man to drive, and we started for Belle Plain landing, nearly thirty miles away. The body was hoisted up the side and swung upon the deck of the "John S. Ide." The morning found us at the dock of the Navy Yard at Washington. LIEUTENANT BAKER.

From the Commandant—Navy Yard
April 27, 1865

Secretary of the Navy
David E. Herold, Prisoner, and the remains of Wilkes Booth were delivered here at 1:45 this morning. The body of Booth is changing rapidly. What disposition shall be made of it? It is now on board the iron-clad "Montauk."
The Secretary of the Navy ordered as follows: Immediately after Surgeon-General Barnes has made his autopsy, you will have the body placed in a strong box and deliver it to the charge of Colonel Baker.

The body was resting upon a rough carpenter's bench, where it had lain since early morning, and it was now awaiting, before a kind of military coroner's jury, an official identification. I found myself mingling with the groups of officials on board. I was soon gazing at the remains, which needed no long inspection to enable me to recognize them. There were missing the moustache and the curling lock upon his forehead. My examination was short, the questions relating to the length of my personal acquaintance with Booth and to the positiveness of my identification. The next witness was Dawson, clerk in the National Hotel, who had known Booth for some years. Presently another witness appeared, Dr. J. Frederick May. As a means of identification he mentioned a tumor on the neck about which he had been consulted. SEATON MONROE.

I examined the body of J. Wilkes Booth after his death, when he was brought to this city. He had a scar upon the large muscle of the left side of his neck, three inches below the ear, occasioned by an operation performed by Dr. May of this city for the removal of a tumor some months previous to Booth's death. It looked like the scar of a burn instead of an incision, which Dr. May explained by the fact that the wound was torn open on the stage when nearly well.

SURGEON–GENERAL J. K. BARNES.

NATIONAL PARK SERVICE

Pictures Found in Booth's Diary

Helen Western

Alice Grey

Bessie Hale

Effie Germon

Fanny Brown

Late in the afternoon of the second day after reaching Washington, Gen. Baker came from the war office and said to me, "The secretary of war wishes me to dispose of Booth's body. He says he don't want the Rebs to get it and make an ado over it. He does not care where it is put, only let it be where it won't be found until Gabriel blows his last trumpet. I want you to go with me."

We started for the navy yard. On the way we would pass the old penitentiary which during the war had been used as an arsenal. Here we stopped and I waited outside while my cousin went in and had a brief interview with the officer in charge; then on to the navy yard. Booth's body was placed in a row boat. We put in a heavy ball and chain and did not try to conceal it from the many watching eyes. One trusty man was in the boat to help us row.

A few touches of the oars and we were half rowing, half drifting down the river. Crowds of people were all along the shore. It went from lip to lip that we had a heavy ball and chain and that, of course, we were going to sink the body. Darkness came on quickly. A couple of miles down the river we quietly ran our boat into a cove in the river bank and rested our oars.

Presently we began pulling slowly back. Soon against the clouded sky we could discern the grim penitentiary walls. The officer in charge was waiting for us. The body was lifted from the boat and carried through the little door to a convict's cell. The stone slab which covered the floor had been lifted and a grave dug under it, and down into the black dismal hole we lowered the once proud, aristocratic, but now despised J. Wilkes Booth. The stone was replaced.

It was believed we had sunk the body in the Potomac and Frank Leslie's paper had a full page cut of Booth's body sliding into the water. LIEUTENANT BAKER.

Post-mortem on the "Saugus" HARPER'S WEEKLY, MAY 13, 1865

FRANK LESLIE'S ILLUSTRATED NEWSPAPER, MAY 20, 1865

The Imagined Burial

(This) sketch was furnished by one of the two officers employed in the duty of sinking the body of Booth in the middle of the Potomac. Although not authorized to divulge his name, I am able to vouch for the truth of the representation. F. LESLIE.

The Actual Burial

FROM BAKER'S HISTORY OF THE U.S. SECRET SERVICE

CHAPTER IX

TRIAL OF THE CENTURY

JUDGMENT

Old Penitentiary
LIBRARY OF CONGRESS

Arrival of Payne

NATIONAL PARK SERVICE

They confined me in a narrow compartment (used as a water closet) aboard an iron clad monitor. The heat was intense. This continued about a week, they not even permitting the cap to be withdrawn, for the purpose of washing. As the silent hour of midnight drew near the dragging and clanking of chains were heard overhead. I felt the tight grasp of some human hand and was roughly conveyed to the deck of the Monitor. It was impossible to learn where I was being conducted, as my head was muffled still in the bag. However, I became aware that I was being conducted upon the gang-plank. Finally she sped on her way, landing me at some unknown point, where I was compelled to walk a long distance, through mud and water.

Arriving at my final destination, the Arsenal, I was thrust into a damp and narrow cell. The canvas bag still remained upon my head, never having allowed its removal to wash my swollen face. The next morning I found myself in the presence of a number of the marshalled heroes of the United States. The charge was read to each by Asst. Judge Advocate Bingham. I was taken back to my cell where I found a differently constructed hood. It fitted the head tightly, containing cotton pads which were directly over the eyes and ears, one small aperture allowed about the nose and one by which food could be served to the mouth. Thus hooded, and doubled ironed I remained day after day, condemned unheard, branded as guilty, before guilt had been established even by that Inquisition Court, a Military Commission, before which I was afterward tried in mockery. This manner of treatment continued uninterrupted, the hoods never being removed excepting when brought before the Court and always replaced on our exit, from about the 25th April to 10th June, 1865. These inflictions and tortures were practiced on nearly all of the others. SAMUEL ARNOLD.

About a mile below Washington, where the high Potomac bluffs meet the marshy border of the Eastern branch, stands the United States Arsenal, a series of long, mathematically uninteresting brick buildings, open to the water, level military plazas, on which are piled pyramids of shell and ball, among acres of cannon and caissons. A high wall, reaching circularly around these buildings, shows above it the barred windows of an older and more gloomy structure than the rest. This has been retransformed to a court-room and jail, and in its third, or uppermost story, the Military Commission is sitting. GEORGE ALFRED TOWNSEND.

FRANK LESLIE'S ILLUSTRATED NEWSPAPER, MAY 26, 1865

Transferring the Prisoners

To avoid self-destruction, each of the prisoners except Mrs. Surratt was compelled to wear a thickly padded hood upon his head, with only holes for his eyes and a slit at the mouth, through which he was fed. The handcuffs consisted of heavy bands about each wrist, connected by a bar ten inches in length; upon his ankles an iron band was riveted, connected by a chain of only sufficient length to permit short steps, and to this chain was attached an iron weight. These manacles upon wrists and ankles were worn continuously, all during imprisonment, night and day.

As the summer advanced the heat became so intense that danger of insanity or death seemed greater than the possibility of self-destruction, and the hoods were removed. By means of daily reports the great secretary of war (Stanton) was in constant touch with every detail, and it was well understood that it was his iron hand that controlled and specified every precaution for the safe keeping of the prisoners.

Mrs. Surratt was never manacled and although always under strict guard, was furnished suitable wholesome food, and at all times, and in all ways was treated with the courtesy, lenity and kindness due her sex. During much of the time she occupied a large airy room on the third floor, and her daughter Anna was frequently permitted to be with her.

R. A. Watts,
assistant adjutant general.

Sam Arnold
as sketched by
General Lew Wallace
COURTESY LEW WALLACE STUDY

HARPER'S WEEKLY, JULY 8, 1865

The Cellblock

We give an accurate and graphic picture of the Old Penitentiary at Washington in which the conspirators are confined and where they have been undergoing trial. There are four rows of cells, which in the picture we give are disclosed to the eye of the reader. No light can enter these cells of confinement but what comes through the windows in the left of the wall.

It is ten o'clock and the court is soon to sit. Its members ride down in superb ambulances and bring their friends along to show them the majesty of justice. A perfect park of carriages stands by the door and from these dismount major generals' wives, in rustling silks; daughters of congressmen, attired like the lilies of the milliner; little girls who hope to be young ladies and have come with "Pa," to look at the assassins; even brides are here, in the fresh blush of their nuptials. These tender creatures have a weakness for the ring of manacles, the sight of folks to be suspended in the air, the face of a woman confederate in blood. George Alfred Townsend.

LIBRARY OF CONGRESS

The Military Commission
Left to right, Col. D.R. Glendenin, Col. C.H. Tomkins, Brig. Gen. T.M. Harris, Brig. Gen. A.D. Howe, Brig. Gen. James A. Ekin, Maj. Gen. Lew Wallace, Maj. Gen. David Hunter, Maj. Gen. A.V. Kautz, Brig. Gen. R.S. Foster, Special Judge Advocate John A. Bingham, Assistant Judge Advocate H.L. Burnett, Judge Advocate General Joseph Holt.

The powers and duties of a military commission are much greater than those of the ordinary jury in a criminal case. This tribunal was a law unto itself. It made its own rules of procedure. It was the sole judge of the law, as well as of the facts. It passed upon the admissibility of all evidence and exceptions to its rulings were not entertained or recorded. It was empowered not only to decide the question of guilt but it also had the power, and it was its duty, to fix the penalties. Only the President of the United States could review, change or modify, approve or disapprove of the findings.

Reverdy Johnson, U. S. Senator from Maryland, one of the leading constitutional lawyers of the country, appeared as counsel for Mrs. Surratt; associated with him were Messrs. Clampitt and Aiken of Washington. General Thomas Ewing, Jr., a son of former Senator Ewing, was retained by Dr. Mudd and Edward Spangler. Frederick Stone of Maryland appeared for Herold. Walter S. Cox, an able attorney of Charles county, was employed by Michael O'Laughlin. Payne and Atzerodt were represented by William E. Doster, a bright young attorney from Baltimore. R. A. Watts.

Before military courts prisoners are presumed to be guilty and are called on to prove their innocence. The prosecution had a month assisted by the whole war power of the Government to get its evidence in shape. The prisoners did not receive their charges until the day the trial opened and then they could only communicate sitting in chains, with a soldier on each side, a great crowd surrounding them, and whisper through the bars to their counsel. The names of the witnesses were not given the prisoners. The crimes were not defined by any known rules of law but were vaguely called offenses against "the common law of war." WILLIAM E. DOSTER,

counsel for Payne and Atzerodt.

The charge and specifications against the defendants were read by Col. Burnett, assistant judge advocate. The substance of the charge against each was: "Maliciously, unlawfully and traitorously, and in aid of the existing armed rebellion against the United States combining, confederating and conspiring together with (naming each defendant) John H. Surratt, John Wilkes Booth, Jefferson Davis, George N. Sanders, Beverly Tucker, Clement C. Clay, Jacob Thompson, and others unknown, to kill and murder Abraham Lincoln, late President, Andrew Johnson, Vice-President, William H. Seward, Secretary of State, and Ulysses S. Grant, then in command of the army of the United States.

The specifications varied. Surratt was specifically charged with harboring, concealing, counseling, aiding and abetting all the defendants. Herold for aiding and assisting Booth to escape, knowing he had assassinated the President. Dr. Mudd was alleged to have aided and assisted the escape of Booth. The specifications against Payne were assaulting, cutting and wounding Secretary Seward with intent to murder. Atzerodt was charged with lying in wait with intent to murder Andrew Johnson. That against O'Laughlin was lying in wait with intent to murder Grant. Spangler was alleged to have aided Booth in reaching the President's box, and guarding the approach, to prevent interference with Booth's attack. Arnold was charged with counseling, combining, and confederating with all of the others. R. A. WATTS.

The appearance and demeanor of the court, it must be admitted, were neither solemn nor impressive. The members of the commission sat about in various negligent attitudes, and a general appearance of disorder was evident. The witnesses were first examined by the judge advocate, the members of the court putting in a question now and then, and the counsel for the prisoners taking up the cross-examination, each counselor attending only to the witness whose testimony affected his own client.

NOAH BROOKS.

The funeral of the President with its million illuminations, its crowds of mourners, its solemn catafalque and processions had just passed. The armies of the Republic were about to be assembled for a triumphal march through the Capitol. These things and the feelings they inspired bore hard against the accused, and could not help dispiriting counsel as much as they encouraged the judge advocate, and tended to inflame the minds of the soldiers who composed the court. WILLIAM E. DOSTER.

HARPER'S WEEKLY, JUNE 10, 1865

The Courtroom

The statement by John A. Bingham that Jefferson Davis is as clearly proven guilty of this conspiracy as John Wilkes Booth, is sufficient indication of the belief in the participation of the confederate government, even among members of the tribunal. This belief gave a wholly misleading bias to the trial at the very outset. It was almost wholly due to the testimony of that terrible liar, Richard Montgomery, who pretended to know leading Southerners, when he said, "We're willing and ready to go to any length to serve the cause of the South." He was later prosecuted for perjury and sentenced to a long imprisonment. Sanford Conover was another of these unmitigated liars. They told hair-raising stories of attempts to introduce clothing infected with yellow fever germs into Northern cities, of a plot to burn New York and many other falsities, which even if they had been true, would have nothing in common with the case.

It is now well known that the leaders of the southern confederacy had no knowledge of the intended conspiracy and had no communication whatever with the actors in the tragedy.

BENN PITMAN,
court recorder.

I satisfied myself that these men were not the originators of the plot but simply tools of men of whom Booth was one & the rebel confederacy the rest. The evid. leaves hardly a doubt that rebel agents were perfectly acqd. with the plot, had agreed with Booth & had money drawn from the Secret Service fund of the confed. to pay for the deed. Add now to this, these horrible disclosures about yellow fever & small pox & the planning under the sanction of the Confed. authorities to sweep the whole country with plague and fire.

E. P. GOODWIN,
a spectator.

The prosecution examined 198 witnesses, the defense 163, a total of 361. The first session was held May 9. The findings and sentences were concluded June 30 and approved by the President July 5, to be carried out July 7.

The court-room was in the third story. It was an apartment about twenty-five feet wide and thirty feet long. Looking into the room, one saw that it was divided lengthwise into two parts, the portion on the right being occupied by the court, sitting around a long, green-covered table, General Hunter at one end, and Judge Advocate General Holt with his assistants at the other. The part of the room which was not occupied by the court was railed off, and was taken up with a few seats for reporters and spectators generally, who were crowded confusedly about, and rested as best they could against the bare, whitewashed walls of the room. At the farther end of the apartment was a wooden railing, behind which, on a narrow, raised platform, sat the accused, all in a solemn row, with an armed soldier sitting between every two persons. Each one of the accused was manacled hand and foot, and sat grimly against the wall, facing the court and the witnesses, the witness-stand being a raised box in the center of the room.

NOAH BROOKS.

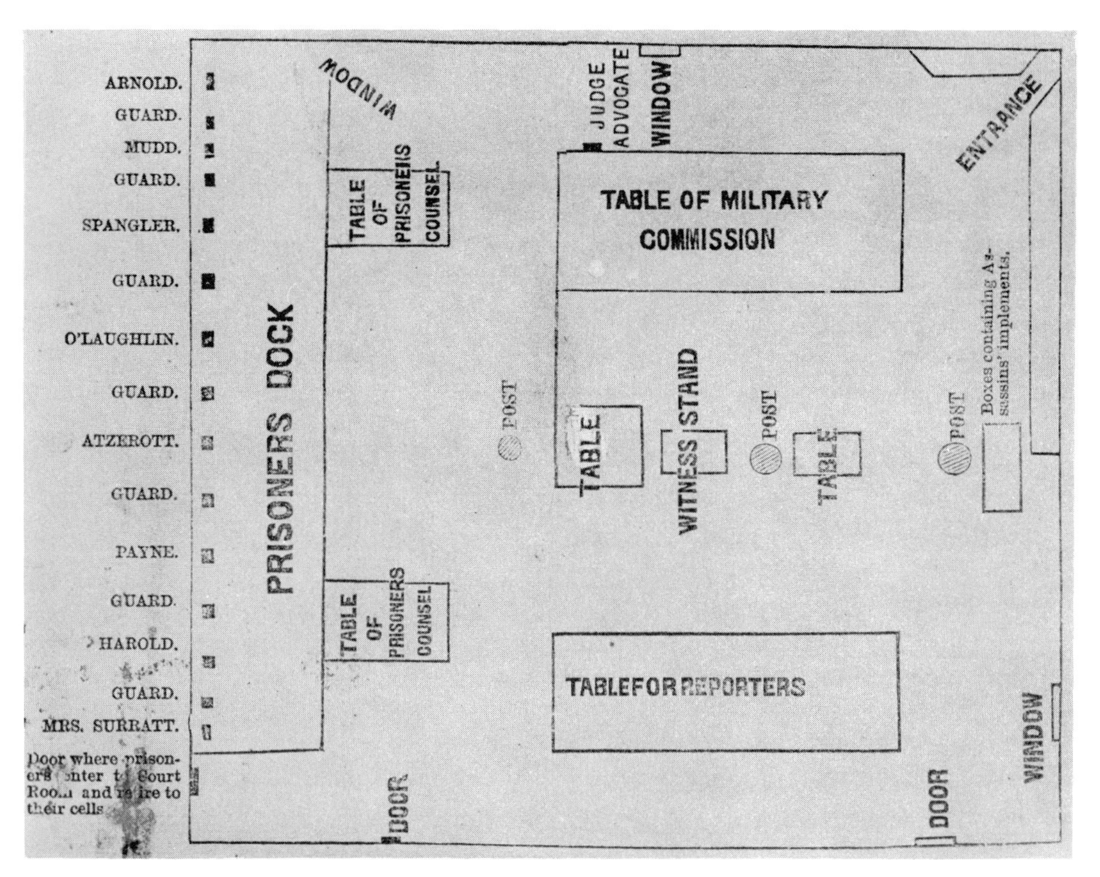

Diagram of Courtroom FROM BENN PITMAN

On the left, sat Mrs. Surratt, deeply veiled, slowly and constantly fanning herself, and never lifting her head except when ordered. She was a dark-looking, fleshy, placid, and matronly woman, apparently about forty-five years of age. She was accused of assisting both before and after the assassination, and secreting in her home the arms and other implements.

Next was Herold, a small, dark man, about twenty-five years old, with a low, receding forehead, scanty black hair and whiskers, a stooping figure, protruding teeth, and a vulgar face. This man was Booth's intimate companion, and left him only when he was burned out in the barn.

Next was Payne, the assassin detailed for the murder of Seward. He sat bolt upright against the wall, looming up like a young giant above all the others. Payne's face would defy the ordinary physiognomist. It certainly appeared to be a good face.

His coarse, black hair was brushed well off his low, broad forehead; his eyes were dark gray, unusually large and liquid. His brawny, muscular chest, which was covered only by a dark, close-fitting "sweater," was that of an athlete. His face, figure, and bearing bespoke him the powerful, resolute creature that he proved to be. It was curious to see the quick flash of intelligence that involuntarily shot from his eyes when the knife with which he had done the bloody work at Seward's house was identified.

Next sat Atzerodt, who had been assigned to the murder of Vice-President Johnson, but whose heart failed him when the time came to strike the blow. This fellow might safely challenge the rest of the party as the completest personification of the low and cunning scoundrel. He was small and sinewy, with long, dark-brown hair, dark-blue and unsteady eyes, a receding, narrow chin and forehead, and a generally villainous countenance.

O'Laughlin, who was supposed to have been set apart for the murder of Stanton or Grant, had the appearance of the traditional stage villain. He had a high, broad forehead, a mass of tangled black hair, a heavy black mustache and chin-whiskers; and his face was blackened by a rough, unshaven beard. His large eyes, black and wild, were never still but appeared to take in everything within the room, scanning each new arrival at the door, watching the witnesses. He often moved his feet, and the clanking of his manacles would attract his attention; he would look down, then back and forth at the scene within the court-room.

Spangler, the stage carpenter of Ford's Theatre, forty, heavily built, sandy complexion, slovenly in appearance. He held Booth's horse at odd times, kept clear the way to the rear of the theater, and was suspected of being his lackey. The poor creature, more than any other, appeared to be under the influence of imminent bodily fear. His hands were incessantly moving along his legs from knee to thigh, his bony fingers traveling back and forth like spiders, as he sat with his eyes fixed on each witness.

Dr. Mudd, the companion and associate of Booth, who received the flying assassin into his house on the night of the murder, and set his fractured limb, in appearance was about thirty-five years of age, with mild blue eyes, a good, broad forehead, ruddy face, hair scanty and thin, a high head, and a sanguine temperament. He sat in his shirt-sleeves, with a white handkerchief knotted loosely about his neck, and attentively regarded the proceedings with the air of a man who felt sure of himself.

Looking out the window was Arnold, the "Sam" of Booth's correspondence, who informed the assassin that he had concluded to "Give up the job," and was tired of keeping up appearances. This man was as uneasy as a caged whelp. He leaned his head on the rail before him, or looked out of the window, or lounged against the wall, or rested his chin on his breast, and generally was absolutely inattentive to everything that went on.

NOAH BROOKS.

The Incriminating Rope
NATIONAL PARK SERVICE

LIBRARY OF CONGRESS
Edwin Spangler

I was standing behind the scenes when someone called out that the President was shot, and directly I saw a man running toward the back door. In a moment I opened the door and the man had got on his horse and was running down the alley. I came back on the stage where I had left Edward Spangler, and he hit me on the face with the back of his hand and said, "Don't say which way he went." I asked him what he meant by slapping me, and he said, "For God's sake shut up."

JACOB RITTERSPAUGH.

After the arrest of Spangler I went to the house where he took his meals. A man at the house handed us a carpetbag, in which we found a piece of rope measuring eighty-one feet.

CHARLES H. ROSCH.

LLOYD OSTENDORF

John W. Clampitt

LLOYD OSTENDORF

William E. Doster

It was in great part by reason of Dr. Mudd's having delayed from Saturday night until Sunday noon to send the authorities at Bryantown information as to the suspected persons who had been at his house, that he was arrested and charged as a conspirator.

GENERAL THOMAS EWING, JR.
counsel for Dr. Mudd and Spangler.

Mudd might just as well have admitted his complicity in the conspiracy. Mudd's expression of countenance was that of a hypocrite. He had the bump of secretiveness largely developed; and it would have taken months of favorable acquaintance to have removed the unfavorable impression made by the first scanning of the man. He had the appearance of a natural born liar and deceiver.

GENERAL T. M. HARRIS,
member of the commission.

The military commission works as if it were delegated not to try but to convict, and Dr. Mudd, if he be innocent, is in only less danger than if he were guilty.

GEORGE ALFRED TOWNSEND.

On the third day of its session, General T. M. Harris, a member of the Commission, objected to the admission of Hon. Reverdy Johnson as counsel (for Mrs. Surratt) before the Commission, on the ground that he did not recognize the moral obligation of an oath designed as a test of loyalty. The Hon. Reverdy Johnson, it was already understood, would in an argument, attack the constitutionality of the Military Commission.

The object of all this was to drive him from the defense, which was successful. Although, after his speech and manner, they dared not openly drive him from the court-room, and therefore rejected the motion of General Harris, yet the object was accomplished; for Senator Johnson, deeply wounded, retired from the court-room and eventually from the case, appearing no more in person, but presenting through the writer his powerful argument on the jurisdiction of the Military Commission.

JOHN W. CLAMPITT,
counsel for Mrs. Surratt.

Reverdy Johnson *General Thomas Ewing, Jr.*

NATIONAL ARCHIVES

LIBRARY OF CONGRESS

Louis J. Weichmann was of Pennsylvania German stock, about twenty-eight years old, tall and broad-shouldered, well educated, speaking several languages, and had been intended for the Catholic priesthood, but had taught school in Washington. Physically and intellectually he was a giant, but in bravery I should call him a dwarf. He boarded at 604 H Street, with Mrs. Surratt, one of whose sons was in the rebel army, and the other, John, with his sister Annie, whom Weichmann admired, lived at home.

D. H. L. Gleason.

Mrs. Surratt had been born and nurtured under the "Old system" in the State of Maryland. In the earlier years of her life she had been a belle in her county; and, at the period when, as her counsel, I had been brought into intimate relations with her, she was still a woman of fine presence and form.

The testimony of Weichmann, the one whom she had nurtured as a son, and who falsely swore her life away to save his own—nowhere reveals the fact that she ever participated in any plot, or was privy to the knowledge that in her house were planned the abduction and final assassination.

From the time Booth gave Weichmann the ten dollars to hire a buggy to convey Mrs. Surratt to Upper Marlborough Court-House, on the day of the assassination, where she went on business connected with her estate, and was made by Booth the innocent bearer of a note and arms to a co-conspirator (Lloyd), who also perjured himself to save his worthless neck, to the second day after the murder of the President, when Lewis Payne, who had made the assault upon the Secretary of State, knocked at her door disguised as a laborer, the chain of the unfortunate circumstances seemed to array itself against the unhappy woman.

These two points were, in fact, the only ones of any importance whatever presented for the prosecution. The commission was organized to convict.

John W. Clampitt.

Louis J. Weichmann
NATIONAL PARK SERVICE

LINCOLN MEMORIAL UNIVERSITY

Mary Eugenia Surratt

Anna Surratt NATIONAL ARCHIVES

Annie Surratt was put on the stand as witness for her mother. It was a pitiable scene. She was tall, slender, fair; for her to stand the stare of the cruel, stony eyes riveted upon her was a trying ordeal. She must have known that her testimony made no impression on that tribunal, and towards the close of it she began to show signs of a collapse. General Hartranft was about to go to her, but knowing her horror of her mother's jailor, he, with delicate consideration, asked me to bring her from the stand.

HENRY KYD DOUGLAS,
witness.

Payne inquired how Mr. Fred Seward was getting along and, when told said he was sorry he had hurt the young man and owed him an apology. His mind seemed of the lowest order, very little above the brute, and his moral faculties equally low. When I saw Payne last in his cell even his fortitude seemed to be shaken by the hurried way he was to be executed. The sentence was read to him on the afternoon of July 6th and he was to be executed the next day. He thanked me heartily for the trouble he had given me and offiered me his jack-knife as the only earthly thing he had to give.

WILLIAM E. DOSTER.

That Mrs. Mary Surratt was entirely innocent of any prior knowledge of, or participation in those crimes, is in my mind beyond question. My conviction is based upon the facts, that as official Recorder of the trial, as having heard every word of testimony, as compiler of the published volume of the "Assassination Trial," and perhaps, more than all, in having, before the trial, written down, from the lips of the principal witnesses, their story of what they knew, or about which in their employment as Spies, they lied, I had the best opportunity of forming a correct judgment of the guilt or innocence of Mrs. Mary Surratt.

Her execution was due solely to the testimony of the drunken tavern keeper, John M. Lloyd, and to the implications of Louis J. Weichmann. That Mrs. Surratt knew of the intentions and plottings of her son, Booth and Atzerodt, to abduct the President, there can be little doubt, but she was wholly innocent of the crime for which she was hanged.

BENN PITMAN.

Benn Pitman
LIBRARY OF CONGRESS

About five o'clock in the afternoon of the 6th of July, while sitting in our office awaiting the findings of the Commission, we were suddenly startled by the cry of the newsboy on the street, "The execution of Mrs. Surratt!" We found to our dismay that, instead of an acquittal, or at most a temporary confinement of our client, the judgment of the Military Commission had been that of death, and the President had signed her death-warrant.

Acting upon the first impulse, we went hastily to the White House, in the hope that Executive clemency might so far intervene as to grant a respite for a few days at least: We were informed that the President would see no one.

Our next movement, was, in company with the daughter, to go the Judge Advocate General. Notwithstanding he had conducted the trial, we thought that, touched by the unutterable woe of the poor girl, the pitying chords of sympathy might find a responsive echo in his heart. Our plea was in vain. Upon her bended knees, bathed in tears, the forlorn girl besought him to go to the President and beg a respite for three days—three days more of life for the mother about to be murdered. Finally, to close the scene, the Judge Advocate General agreed to meet us at the Executive Mansion at a given hour. We reached there at the appointed time. He had gone before us, and was just emerging as we came. He said: "I can do nothing. The President is immovable. He has carefully examined the findings of the Commission and has no reason to change the date of execution."

We left in despair, and telegraphed Hon. Reverdy Johnson, requesting his immediate presence. He telegraphed the following reply: "It is very late. There are no trains to Washington City. Apply for a writ of habeas corpus and take her body from the custody of the military authorities. We are now in a state of peace—not war." We determined to make the attempt, and although past midnight, proceeded to prepare the petition. We never for a moment doubted the efficacy of the writ, could we prevail upon its issue.

President Andrew Johnson
NATIONAL ARCHIVES

Judge Advocate General Joseph Holt
NATIONAL ARCHIVES

We drove immediately to the residence of Hon. Andrew Wylie, and, just as the clock tolled the hour of two in the morning, rung the front bell. The Judge listened attentively to each sentence of our petition, which was of some length. "I believe it my duty, as a judge, to order this writ to issue," and at four in the morning we placed it in the hands of the United States Marshal, with the request that it be served immediately upon General Hancock, the commandant of the military district. The Marshal served the writ upon Hancock. The President and his ill advisers, believing that General Hancock would undoubtedly obey the writ, assumed the illegal authority of suspending it.

All hope faded, and we proceeded to the Arsenal to take a last farewell of the doomed woman. On our way we noticed cavalrymen stationed at points along the line from the White House to the Arsenal. These were stationed by General Hancock to speed the tidings, should the President at the last moment relent.

It was at first proposed (and I have it from most credible authority) to acquit Mrs. Surratt, or at least to spare her life. To this the Judge Advocate General objected, and in its stead proposed that the Commission render the same judgment as in the cases of Payne, Atzerodt, and Herold, with a recommendation (for clemency) drawn and signed by a majority of the Commission.

Andrew Johnson averred upon his honor that he never saw that recommendation until two years after the execution, when sending for the papers in the case, he found it among them in a detached form. It is doubtless true that the recommendation for mercy was not placed before the President with the findings of the Commission at the time they were presented for his approval (by Holt), but was retained by those in authority, who sought the blood of the innocent woman. JOHN W. CLAMPITT.

The character of Mr. Johnson shows more clearly why these people were summarily hanged. His obstinacy and self-will when opposed by appeals for mercy or magnanimity of sentiment carried him to the opposite extreme of rigor. The suspicion that he might have been one of them made him hasten to show by severity that his hands were clean. WILLIAM E. DOSTER.

About half-past eight this morning, Miss Surratt again visited the White House, for the purpose of obtaining an interview with the President. The door-keeper stopped her at the foot of the steps leading up to the President's office. Miss Surratt threw herself upon the stair steps, where she remained a considerable time, sobbing aloud in the greatest anguish, protesting her mother's innocence, and imploring every one who came near to intercede in her mother's behalf, but at last, she drove again to the jail and lay in her mother's cell.

On Monday, Mudd, Arnold, O'Laughlin, and Spangler, will go northward to prison. The three former for life, the last for six years.

Close by at the foot of the gallows four wooden boxes were piled upon each other at the edge of four newly excavated pits, the fresh earth of which was already dried and brittle in the burning noon. They were so placed that as the victims should emerge from the gaol door they would be seen near the stair directly in the line of march.

Suddenly the wicket opens. First came a woman pinioned. A middle-aged woman, dressed in black, bonnetted and veiled, walking between two bare-headed priests. One of these held against his breast a crucifix, both of them muttered the service for the dead. Four soldiers with musket at shoulder followed, and a captain led the way to the gallows.

The second escorted a small and shambling German, whose head had a long white cap upon it, rendering more filthy his dull complexion, and upon whose feet the chains

The Graves LIBRARY OF CONGRESS

LIBRARY OF CONGRESS *Reading the Sentences*

clanked as he slowly advanced, preceded by two officers, flanked by a Lutheran clergyman.

The third, preacher and party, clustered about a shabby boy, whose limbs tottered as he progressed.

The fourth walked in the shadow of a straight high stature, whose tawny hair and large blue eyes were suggestive rather of the barbarian striding in his conqueror's triumph, than the assassin going to the gallows.

All these, captives, priests, guards and officers, nearly twenty in all, climbed slowly the narrow steps; and upon four arm chairs, the condemned were seated with their

Adjusting the Noose
LIBRARY OF CONGRESS

spiritual attendants behind them. The findings and warrants were read to the prisoners by General Hartranft.

At first she was very feeble, and leaned her head upon alternate sides of her armchair in nervous spasms, but now and then, when a sort of wail issued from her lips, the priest placed before her the crucifix to lull her fearful spirit. She wore a robe of dark woolen, no collar, and common shoes of black listing. Her general expression was that of acute suffering. Her base and fugitive son, to know the infamy of his cowardice and die of his shame, should have seen his mother writhing in her seat upon the throne his wickedness established for her.

Payne, the strangest criminal in our history, was alone dignified and self-possessed. He wore a closely fitting knit shirt, a sailor's straw hat tied with a ribbon, and dark pantaloons, but no shoes. His collar showed the tremendous muscularity of his neck, and the breadth of his breast was more conspicuous by the manner in which his pinioned arms thrust it forward. His height, his vigor, his glare made him the strong central figure of this tableau. He was only looking at death as for one long expected.

The third condemned, although whimpering, had far more grit than I would have expected. He was inquisitive and flippant-faced. Herold would have enjoyed this execution vastly as a spectator. He was, I think, capable of a greater degree of depravity than any of his accomplices. In his dirty felt hat, soiled cloth coat, light pantaloons and stockings, he seemed unworthy of his manacles.

Atzerodt was my ideal of a man to be hung, with his muttering to the air, and a pallidness transparent through his dirt as he jabbered prayers and pleas confusedly. He wore a greyish coat, black vest, light pantaloons and slippers. Atzerodt lost his life through too much gabbing. These were the dramatis personae. They were altogether a motley and miserable set. GEORGE ALFRED TOWNSEND.

During her execution, her daughter Anna was present in a room on the second floor of the Arsenal. She sat at one window and I at another, which windows commanded the yard. She stood at one of the windows until the rope was fixed. Then she fell down in a swoon. WILLIAM E. DOSTER.

When Hancock failed to put in an appearance, I was sure Mrs. Surratt would be saved. But at last he came, and turning to me said: "All is ready, Captain; proceed." I said to him "Her, too?" "Yes," he said: "she cannot be saved." When the nooses had been adjusted and the caps pulled over the heads, before I gave the signal to the men below to knock the posts from under the drop, I stepped up to Payne, tightened his noose under the cap, and said, "Payne, I want you to die quick"; to which he replied in a soft voice without a single tremor: "You know best, Captain." I gave the signal, the two drops fell with a sickening thud, and, as one, the four bodies shot down and hung in mid-air. After twenty minutes Major Porter pronounced them dead.

CHRISTIAN RATH.

Final Scene (*next page*)
LIBRARY OF CONGRESS

This trial settled nothing. It led to four executions but a lynching would have done that. The certainty of guilt upon well-defined and known crimes on which our notions of justice rest was never had. And the haste with which the condemned were dispatched shows an unfair discrimination and a heat of passion utterly unlike the calm and fair features of eternal justice. WILLIAM E. DOSTER.

The trial and swift punishment of these execrable assassins was of the utmost importance. The excitement throughout all the land, north and south, was intense. The very air in and about Washington was murky with suspicion; whispers and rumors of contemplated assassinations were everywhere. It may well be said that the country at large might have suffered far greater by temporizing, quibblings and delays than by any technical infraction on the strict interpretation of the constitution. At that time it was patent to everyone that a trial of these people before a jury impanelled in the District of Columbia would have failed to convict. The trial and failure to convict John H. Surratt for the same offense two years later, before a civil jury, verified the wisdom of the military tribunal in this case. R. A. WATTS.

The Military Commission had fulfilled its mission, the death of Abraham Lincoln had been avenged, the public's cry for vengeance had been appeased, and the long-drawn-out trial, which for two months had heaped fuel to the fire to add to the public excitement, passed out of existence and the Nation at large became pacified.

SAMUEL ARNOLD.

Surratt Grave CLAUDE SIMMONS

NOTES

This work consists of quotations taken directly from the sources. In many instances the original material has been abridged to meet the requirements of space or to avoid redundancy. However, the statements as printed have not been paraphrased, but rather condensed through deletion of nonessential passages. This has necessitated some revision of punctuation and capitalization, but the sequence of thought, grammar, and spelling are unchanged from the original. Customary practice of using the ellipsis to denote omissions has not been followed.

Chapter I

Page 14: Ben Perley Poore, *The Conspiracy Trial for the Murder of the President,* Vol. 1 (Boston, J. E. Tilton and Company, 1865), p. 195. The last day of the President's life is dramatically presented in Jim Bishop, *The Day Lincoln Was Shot* (Harper, 1955). An earlier work is John W. Starr, Jr., *Lincoln's Last Day* (Stokes, 1922), and Mrs. Lincoln's account is found in Honoré Willsie Morrow, "Lincoln's Last Day," *Cosmopolitan* (February, 1930), pp. 31 ff.

Page 15: Campbell MacCulloch, "This Man Saw Lincoln Shot," *Good Housekeeping* (February, 1927), p. 20. Lincoln's interest in the theater and particularly in Shakespearean productions and actors is well known. Sandburg has written relative to this in some detail. The topic is discussed also in Leonard Grover, "Lincoln's Interest in the Theater," *Century Magazine* (April, 1909); R. Hanser, "Lincoln Loved a Show," *Theater Arts* (February, 1959); and Art Hemminger, *Mr. Lincoln Goes to the Theatre* (Poor Richard Press), 1941.

Page 16:
A. Helen DuBarry, "Eyewitness Account of Lincoln's Assassination," *Journal of the Illinois State Historical Society,* Vol. 39 (September, 1946), pp. 366–67.

B. W. J. Ferguson, *I Saw Booth Shoot Lincoln* (Boston, Houghton Mifflin, 1930), pp. 23–4. For a definitive treatment of the history of Ford's and the ambitious project of restoration of this significant shrine, consult George J. Olszewski, *Restoration of Ford's Theatre* (National Park Service, 1963). When completed in late 1966 the 2.7 million dollar project will have recreated the playhouse exactly as it was in 1865, when it was regarded as one of the finest in the nation. See also *Lincoln Lore* (November 9, 1953).

Page 17: Affidavit from B. F. Morris, *Memorial Record of the Nation's Tribute to Abraham Lincoln* (Washington, W. H. & O. H. Morrison, 1865), p. 42. Tireless researcher Otto Eisenschiml (*In the Shadow of Lincoln's Death*) saw an ominous connotation in the almost identical language used by Rathbone in his three statements given over a three-year period.

Page 18:
A. *Ibid.,* p. 43. The story of this historically interesting item now at Greenfield Village is related in Kenneth M. Metcalf, "Biography of a Chair," *Lincoln Herald* (Winter 1961). See also H. E. Bower, "Lincoln's Chair in Ford's Museum," *Saturday Review of Literature* (March 3, 1934).

B. William H. Crook, "Lincoln's Last Day," *Harper's Monthly* (September, 1907), pp. 527–28. The ineptness of contemporary officialdom is nowhere better evidenced than in its failure to investigate and punish Parker for his catastrophic negligence. There remains today an incredible air of mystery as to why a character of so unsavory a record should have been assigned a post of such responsibility. Little was said of him following the assassination but in 1936 the research of Kimmel uncovered the odious background of the wretch. This material was developed into a chapter-length treatment in Otto Eisenschiml, *Why Was Lincoln Murdered?* A later appraisal of John F. Parker is Jack Kofoed, "The Man Who Helped Kill Lincoln," *Argosy* (February, 1959). Almost unbelievably, Mrs. Lincoln, in her ignorance of Parker's ill repute, was instrumental in his appointment as guard.

Page 20:
A. John Gilmary Shea, *The Lincoln Memorial: A Record of the Life, Assassination, and Obsequies of the Martyred President* (New York, Bunce & Huntington, 1865), pp. 65–66.

B. Julia Adelaide Shepard, "Lincoln's Assassination Told by an Eye-Witness," *Century Magazine* (April, 1909), p. 917. A modern audience would fail to understand the singular success enjoyed by *Our American Cousin* a century ago. Theatrical fame and fortune came to Laura Keene, Joseph Jefferson and E. A. Sothern following their roles in Tom Taylor's eccentric comedy. The vehicle, regarded as Miss Keene's personal property, had seen her in more than one thousand performances as Florence Trenchard.

Page 21: Shea, *op. cit.*, p. 66.

Page 22: Morris, *loc. cit.*

Page 23: Charles Sabin Taft, "Abraham Lincoln's Last Hours," *Century Magazine* (February, 1893), p. 634.

Page 24:
A. Morris, *op. cit.*, p. 44.

B. *Ibid.*, p. 43.

Page 25: Benn Pitman, *Assassination of the President and the Trial of the Conspirators* (Cincinnati, Moore, Wilstach & Baldwin, 1865), p. 76. James Ferguson was the only person to see the President at almost the precise fatal moment, and his testimony that Lincoln seemed to be looking down and to his left explains how the wound could be on the left side of the head instead of the right, as would have been expected from his normal position in the box. Whether Booth shouted *"Sic semper tyrannis,"* or something else, or nothing, has never been established with certainty.

Page 26:
A. Shea, *op. cit.*, p. 64.

B. Ferguson, *op. cit.*, p. 37.

C. Pitman, *op. cit.*, p. 79.

Page 27: Charles A. Leale, *Address Delivered Before the Commandery of the State of N. Y. Military Order of the Loyal Legion of the U. S.*, February, 1909. Leale's first report of the night's events are found in his letter to General Benjamin F. Butler in 1867, "Butler papers," Library of Congress. This is discussed in Hans Louis Trefousse, "Belated Revelations of the Assassination Committee," *Lincoln Herald* (Spring-Summer, 1956), pp. 13 ff.

Page 28:
A. Taft, *op. cit.*, p. 635.

B. Jesse W. Weik, "A New Story of Lincoln's Assassination," *Century Magazine* (February, 1913), pp. 559–62.

C. Pitman, *loc. cit.*

Page 29: Leale, *op. cit.* Leale's efforts in mouth-to-mouth breathing are discussed in J. Willard Montgomery, M.D., "Resuscitation of President Lincoln," *Journal of the American Medical Association* (April 8, 1961).

Page 30: Seaton Monroe, "Recollections of Lincoln's Assassination," *North American Review* (April, 1896), p. 434.

Page 31:
A. Leale, *op. cit.*

B. Poore, *op. cit.*, p. 413.

C. Pitman, *op. cit.*, p. 82. The fatal weapon was a single-shot derringer, slightly less than six inches in length and weighing half a pound. A muzzle loader, it fired a ball one-half inch in diameter by means of a brass percussion cap.

Pages 32–33: Frederick W. Seward, "Recollections of Lincoln's Last Hours," *Leslie's Illustrated Weekly* (February 4, 1909), p. 107. All the victims of Payne's sanguinary attack recovered. However, Frederick Seward was incapacitated for months and the wife of the Secretary, who was in ill health, suffered shock and died shortly after this ghastly experience. A medical man's appraisal of the event is John K. Lattimer, M.D., "The Stabbing of Lincoln's Secretary of State on the Night the President Was Shot," *Journal of the American Medical Association* (April 12, 1965).

Chapter II

Page 36: Dorothy Hemenway Van Ark, "New Light on Lincoln's Death," *Saturday Evening Post* (February 12, 1944), p. 82. Excerpts from a letter discovered in 1944 which reveals the identity of the other main-floor occupants and also explains, by inference, why the physicians bypassed the nearer and much larger bedroom in preference for the smaller back room where the bed was "made up."

Page 37:
A. Leale, *op. cit.,* p. 7. Many claimed the distinction of helping carry the President on this short, somber journey. However, the account of the four Pennsylvania artillerymen has the simple sound of truth. This is related in the *New York Times* (February 8, 1931), and is quoted in Carl Sandburg, *Abraham Lincoln,* Vol. VI, p. 286.

B. Van Ark, *loc. cit.*

C. Leale, *op. cit.,* p. 8. At least thirteen physicians were in attendance to some degree during the night, including those present in the box, Leale, Taft, and King. Also present were the Surgeon-General, Assistant Surgeon-General and Acting Assistant Surgeon-General, as well as the family physician, Dr. Stone. Leale and Taft held the rank of Assistant Surgeon, U.S. Volunteers. The complete list is found in *Lincoln Lore* (April 14, 1941).

D. Taft, *loc. cit.* Other Taft accounts are found in *Medical Record* (April 1, 1893); New York *Tribune* (August 12, 1900); *Minnesota Medicine* (February, 1948).

E. Morris, *op. cit.,* p. 43.

Page 38:
A. General L. C. Baker, *History of the United States Secret Service* (Philadelphia, L. C. Baker, 1867), p. 469. National Park Service states the precise measurements of the bedroom were 18 feet 2 inches by 9 feet 11 inches. Rockwell's diagram lists twenty-one persons as present at the hour of death. However, the exact number of visitors to the room during the night may never be known. Bachelder's "official" painting portrays forty-six people, but others are known to have been present. *Lincoln Lore* (November 6, 1950) lists fifty-one names, but this is not complete. The question is discussed in Eisenschiml, *Why Was Lincoln Murdered?,* p. 480. It will be noted that Rockwell's steps are incorrectly drawn.

B. *Frank Leslie's Illustrated Newspaper* (April 29, 1865). Nearly all sketches of the assassination scenes were the work of Berghaus.

C. Pitman, *op. cit.,* p. 81. It is sometimes asked if modern medical science could have saved the President's life. The answer is an emphatic "No." Surgeons in attendance were instantaneous and unanimous as to the terminal nature of the wound. Present-day judgment is in agreement, as seen in Otto Eisenschiml, *The Case of A----L----, Aged 56,* and his "Could Lincoln Have Been Saved?" in *Coronet* (April, 1941). An exceptionally complete recent article is John K. Latimer, M.D., "The Wound That Killed Lincoln," *Journal of the American Medical Association* (February 15, 1964).

D. Hugh McCulloch, *Men and Measures of Half a Century* (New York, Charles Scribner's Sons, 1900), p. 224.

E. Rufus Rockwell Wilson, *Lincoln Among His Friends* (Caldwell, Idaho, Caxton Printers, 1942), p. 385. Gobright, with more than thirty years of experience in Washington journalism behind him, wrote an account of the night's events that is unsurpassed in lucidity and scope.

Page 40:
A. Charles A. Dana, *Lincoln and His Cabinet* (De Vinne Press, 1896), p. 68. Stanton's detractors have held that rather than dictating numerous verbose reports, he could have with greater purpose sent a pursuit party to the obvious escape point, the Navy Yard bridge.

B. Moorfield Storey, "Dickens, Stanton, Sumner, and Storey," *Atlantic Monthly* (April, 1930), p. 465. Johnson's critics have contended the Vice-President did not call at the Petersen house. This statement by Stanton, no Johnson admirer, substantiates other evidence of his presence. The question has been recently explored and thoroughly resolved in *Lincoln Lore* (July, 1964). Upon hearing the tragic news, Sumner mistakenly rushed to the White House where he was the first to inform the household. Robert Lincoln, who had been chatting with John Hay, hurried downstairs to join the senator in a fast ride to the Petersen house. Younger son Tad was seeing a performance of *Aladdin* at Grover's.

C. Taft, *loc. cit.*

Page 41:

A. Gideon Welles, *Diary of Gideon Welles,* Vol. II (Boston, Houghton Mifflin, 1909), p. 287.

B. Leale, *op. cit.,* p. 9.

C. *Lincoln Lore,* April, 1961.

Page 42:

A. Crook, *op. cit.*

B. Leale, *op. cit.,* p. 11.

Page 43:

A. Welles, *loc. cit.*

B. Taft, *loc. cit.* Ritchie's work is one of the three best-known paintings of the death scene. Stefan Lorant, authority on Lincoln pictures, shows the three in his *Lincoln: His Life in Photographs* (New York: Duell, Sloan & Pearce, 1941). There were numerous portrayals of the scene in the lithographs of the time, none distinguished for its historical or artistic qualities. Ten death scenes appeared in *Lincoln Lore* (July, 1964).

C. D. R. Barbee, "President Lincoln and Doctor Gurley," *Abraham Lincoln Quarterly,* Vol. 5 (March, 1948), pp. 20–21.

D. John G. Nicolay and John Hay, "The Fourteenth of April," *Century Magazine* (January, 1890), p. 436. Otto Eisenschiml, whose distrust of Stanton was boundless, vigorously attacked the authenticity of Hay's recollection of this enduring and classic utterance in *Why Was Lincoln Murdered?,* p. 483.

Page 46:

A. Welles, *op. cit.,* p. 288.

B. Ferguson, *op. cit.,* p. 54.

C. Baker, *op. cit.,* p. 470.

D. James Tanner, "At the Bedside of Abraham Lincoln," *National Republic* (August, 1926), p. 34.

E. Smith Stimmel, "Experiences as a Member of President Lincoln's Bodyguard," *North Dakota Historical Review* (January, 1927), p. 31.

Page 48:

A. Morris, *op. cit.,* p. 41. The autopsy was performed at the White House. It is discussed in detail in Eisenschiml, *The Case of A----L----, Aged 56.*

B. Pitman, *op. cit.,* p. 82.

Page 49: Osborn H. Oldroyd, *The Assassination of Abraham Lincoln* (Washington, O. H. Oldroyd, 1910), p. 37. Clark was a private in Company D, 13th Massachusetts Infantry. One of two spectacular assassination photographs uncovered in recent years was that of the blood-stained bed, as dramatically revealed in Dorothy Meserve Kuhnhardt, "Lincoln Died Here Two Hours Before," *Life* (April 14, 1961). Squeamish moderns probably consider such grisly desire for souvenirs incomprehensible, but apparently it was accepted behavior at the time. Albert Daggett, who lived next door, wrote proudly of his blood-stained relics (*Lincoln Lore,* April, 1961), and George Francis (Van Ark, *op. cit.*) tells about the enterprising young men who filched Mrs. Lincoln's hat to be cut up as souvenirs.

Chapter III

Page 52: Noah Brooks, "The Close of Lincoln's Career," *Century Magazine* (May, 1895), p. 23.

Page 53: "Lincoln's Death," *The Collector* (March, 1950), pp. 49–50.

Page 54:
A. Orville Hickman Browning, *The Diary of Orville Hickman Browning,* Vol. 2, Illinois State Historical Library Collections, p. 20. Browning, one of Lincoln's political cronies, had completed the unexpired portion of Douglas' term in the Senate, where he was regarded as the President's voice. At this time he was a successful influence peddler.
B. Shea, *op. cit.,* p. 111. The embalming process is explained in *Lincoln Lore* (May, 1958).
C. Welles, *op. cit.,* p. 292.

Page 55: Milton H. Schutes, *Lincoln and the Doctors, a Medical Narrative of the Life of Abraham Lincoln* (Elmira, N.Y., Pioneer Press, 1933), p. 132. There was a sorrowful sequel to this touching letter. Only three months later Dr. Henry lost his life when the *Brother Jonathan* sank two days out of San Francisco.

Page 57: John G. Nicolay and John Hay, "The Mourning Pageant," *Century Magazine* (January, 1890), p. 439.

Page 58:
A. William T. Coggeshall, *The Journeys of Abraham Lincoln: From Springfield to Washington, 1861, as President Elect and from Washington to Springfield, 1865 as President Martyred* (Columbus, Ohio State Journal, 1865), p. 107.
B. *Daily Pantograph* (Bloomington, Illinois), April 18, 1865. As is well known, the thousands of sermons prepared for a jubilant first Sunday of peace were discarded to be replaced by gloomy discourses throughout the North. Vindictiveness characterized many of these and some pastors deplored Lincoln's presence at a theater on Good Friday. A scholarly treatment of this topic is Jay Monaghan, "An Analysis of Lincoln's Funeral Sermons," *Indiana Magazine of History* (March, 1945).

Page 60:
A. Elizabeth Keckley, *Behind the Scenes* (New York, G. W. Carlton & Co., 1868), p. 187. Mrs. Keckley was a mulatto seamstress who became Mrs. Lincoln's nurse, maid and confidante, as well as dressmaker.
B. Browning, *op. cit.,* p. 22.
C. Brooks, *loc. cit.* At the time of President Kennedy's death it was reported that his widow requested aides to check data on the Lincoln funeral.
D. Coggeshall, *op. cit.,* p. 110.

Pages 60–61: M. Helen Palmes Moss, "Lincoln and Wilkes Booth on the Day of the Assassination," *Century Magazine* (April, 1909), p. 953.

Page 61: Morris, *op. cit.,* p. 74.

Page 63:
A. *Ibid.,* p. 94.
B. James D. Richardson, *Messages and Papers of the Presidents,* Vol. 6 (Washington, Bureau of National Literature and Art, 1909), p. 294.

Pages 64–65: George Alfred Townsend, *The Life, Crime, and Capture of John Wilkes Booth* (New York, Dick & Fitzgerald, 1865), p. 14. This short work, compiled largely from his daily dispatches, is an almost inexhaustible source book for historians of this period. He was widely copied by his contemporaries, invariably without credit.

Page 65: *Harper's Weekly* (May 6, 1865). All contemporary sketches of the White House ceremonies erroneously show the presence of a woman. The distraught widow, devastated by shock, was possessed of an overwhelming grief, and remained in complete seclusion, seeing almost no one except Mrs. Welles and Mrs. Keckley. Five weeks after the assassination she left Washington accompanied by her two sons, Mrs. Keckley and Crook, making the sad and tedious fifty-four hour journey to Chicago. There was no thought of returning to Springfield.

Pages 68–69: Townsend, *op. cit.,* p. 18.

Page 70: *Ibid.,* p. 17.

Page 72: Morris, *op. cit.,* p. 101.

Page 73: Shea, *op. cit.,* p. 134.

Page 74:
A. *Ibid.,* p. 135.

B. Townsend, *op. cit.,* p. 18. Ninety-eight years later the body of assassinated President Kennedy reposed on this same catafalque.

Pages 74–75: Coggeshall, *op. cit.,* p. 135.

Page 75:
A. Noah Brooks, *Washington in Lincoln's Time* (New York, The Century Company, 1894), p. 265.

B. Welles, *op. cit.,* p. 293.

Chapter IV

Page 78: Major General E. D. Townsend, *Anecdotes of the Civil War* (New York, Appleton and Company, 1884), p. 221.

Page 79:
A. Shea, *op. cit.,* p. 167. In the train party were the military, senators, congressmen and governors, as well as other officials. The largest group was that from Illinois. Names of those leaving Washington and the official orders for the operation of the train are found in Morris, *op. cit.* Representing the War Department in charge of the train was Brigadier General E. D. Townsend.

B. Morris, *op. cit.,* p. 106.

Page 80:
A. Chicago *Times,* May 2, 1865.

B. Coggeshall, *op. cit.,* p. 138.

Page 81: Chicago *Times, loc. cit.* Following the war the government, with high disregard for historical values, disposed of the funeral coach. It suffered various forms of humiliation until finally destroyed by fire in Minneapolis in 1911. For the full story of the car see *Lincoln Lore* (May, 1957). A shorter account is Carl R. Gray, *The Lincoln Car on the Union Pacific* (Princeton University Press, 1937).

Page 82: D. B. Williamson, *Illustrated Life, Services, Martyrdom and Funeral of Abraham Lincoln* (Philadelphia, T. B. Peterson and Brothers, 1865), p. 230.

Page 83:
A. Baltimore *American* (April 21, 1865).

B. Harrisburg *Patriot and Union* (April 21, 1865).

C. Isaac N. Arnold, *The History of Abraham Lincoln and the Overthrow of Slavery* (Chicago, Clark & Company, 1866), p. 669. The reception in Baltimore was in vast contrast to that accorded Lincoln in February, 1861. The first passage through the city and the enigmatic events of that time are found in Norma B. Cuthbert, *Lincoln and the Baltimore Plot* (The Huntington Library, 1949).

Page 84: Harrisburg *Patriot and Union* (April 22, 1865).

Page 85: *Ibid.*

Page 86:
A. Harry E. Pratt (compiler), *Concerning Mr. Lincoln* (Springfield, The Abraham Lincoln Association, 1944), p. 125.

B. Williamson, *op. cit.,* p. 234.

Pages 86–87: Coggeshall, *op. cit.,* p. 151.

Page 88:
A. Williamson, *op. cit.,* p. 238.

B. Philadelphia *Inquirer* (April 24, 1865).

Pages 88–89: Pratt, *op. cit.,* pp. 126 ff.

Pages 90–91: Coggeshall, *op. cit.,* pp. 159 ff.

Page 92: Ibid.

Page 95:
A. *Ibid.* The discovery of this photograph showing Lincoln in his casket was a sensational event among Lincoln students. It was first published in *Life* (September 15, 1952), with an accompanying article by Stefan Lorant. The complete story of the long-lost picture and its discovery by a fifteen year old boy at Illinois State Historical Library is told in *Lincoln Lore* (September 22, 1952). A photograph published on the same subject by *Saturday Evening Post* (February 15, 1941), was found to be spurious.

B. David T. Valentine, *Obsequies of Abraham Lincoln in the City of New York* (New York, Edmund Jones & Company, 1866), p. 128.

Page 96: Shea, *op. cit.,* p. 185. One of the children shown in this picture is Theodore Roosevelt. The photograph and story were published in *American Heritage* (June, 1955), by Stefan Lorant, who made the discovery. The title is "The Boy in the Window."

Page 97: Valentine, *op. cit.,* p. 149.

Page 98: Ibid., p. 129.

Page 99:
A. Coggeshall, *op. cit.,* p. 171.

B. Morris, *op. cit.,* p. 167.

Page 101: New York *Herald* (April 26, 1865).

Page 102:
A. Coggeshall, *op. cit.,* p. 197.

B. E. D. Townsend, *op. cit.,* p. 233.

C. Morris, *op. cit.,* p. 180.

Page 103:
A. Albany *Atlas & Argus* (April 27, 1865).

B. Chauncey M. Depew, *My Memories of Eighty Years* (New York, Scribner's, 1922), p. 65.

Page 105: Buffalo *Morning Express* (April 28, 1865).

Page 106: Cleveland *Leader* (April 29, 1865).

Pages 108–109: Columbus *Gazette* (May 5, 1865).

Pages 110–111: Indianapolis *Daily Sentinel* (May 1, 1865).

Page 112:
A. Indianapolis *Daily Journal* (April 30, 1865).

B. Morris, *op. cit.,* p. 142.

Pages 113–119: Chicago *Times* (May 2, 1865). *Lincoln Lore* (May, 1962).

Page 119: New York Times (May 3, 1865).

Chapter V

Page 122: Pratt, *op. cit.,* p. 129. Bromwell did not exaggerate; the civic pride of Springfield was mortally wounded. Only when Mrs. Lincoln threatened to take the body elsewhere, did the people give grudging consent to Oak Ridge. There is evidence the widow was acting on the desires of the President in the matter. Understandably, too, she wished to be assured the place selected would later have room for her body. The full story of this unseemly affair is related in Paul M. Angle, "The Building of the Lincoln Monument," *Lincoln Centennial Association Papers* (February, 1926). How Lincoln's last request was fulfilled is told in *Lincoln Lore* (May 28, 1945).

Page 123: Henry B. Rankin, *Intimate Character Sketches of Abraham Lincoln* (New York, J. B. Lippincott Company, Copyright 1924, 1952 by Emma R. Barber), p. 317. Rankin studied law in the Lincoln-Herndon office.

Page 124:
A. Edmond Beall, "Recollections of the Assassination and Funeral of Abraham Lincoln," *Journal of the Illinois State Historical Society,* Vol. 5 (January, 1913), pp. 488–92.

B. W. W. Sweet, "Bishop Simpson and the Funeral of Abraham Lincoln," *Journal of the Illinois State Historical Society,* Vol. 7 (April, 1914), pp. 62–71.

Page 125: Illinois State Journal (May 4, 1865). The most complete account of the Springfield obsequies is found in John Carroll Power, *Abraham Lincoln, His Life, Public Services, etc.* (H. W. Rokker, 1889).

Page 126:
A. William S. Porter, "The Lincoln Funeral Train," *Journal of the Illinois State Historical Society,* Vol. 9 (October, 1916), pp. 315–19.

B. *Illinois State Journal, loc. cit.*

Page 127:
A. William Henry Herndon and Jesse W. Weik, *Herndon's Life of Lincoln* (Cleveland, World Publishing Company, 1930), p. 461. Lincoln's partnership with controversial "Billy" Herndon was formed in 1844 and continued until the President's death.

B. *Illinois State Journal, loc. cit.*

Page 130:
A. *Ibid.* The hearse had been built in Philadelphia at a cost of $6,000.

B. Sweet, *loc. cit.* The exhibitions netted the purchaser over $25,000. The tainted transaction is described in *Life of Abraham Lincoln* (Mast, Crowell & Kirkpatrick, 1896).

Page 132: Coggeshall, *op. cit.,* p. 303. Unfortunately most present-day visitors to Oak Ridge fail to visit the secluded spot, which remains much as it was on the day of the funeral.

Page 133:
A. *Illinois State Journal* (May 6, 1865). For the bizarre story of the Lincoln tomb ghouls see John Carroll Power, *History of an Attempt to Steal the Body of Abraham Lincoln, etc.* (H. W. Rokker Printing and Publishing House, 1890). A more readable account is Lloyd Lewis, *Myths After Lincoln* (Harcourt, Brace and Company, 1929).

B. Edward L. Merritt, "Recollections of the Part Springfield Bore in the Obsequies of Abraham Lincoln," *Illinois Historical Society Transactions* (1909), pp. 179–83.

Chapter VI

Page 138:
A. Unidentified clipping.

B. Quoted in Francis Wilson, *John Wilkes Booth* (Boston, Houghton Mifflin, 1929), pp. 82–83.

C. J. E. Buckingham, Sr., *Reminiscences of the Assassination of Abraham Lincoln* (Washington, Press of Rufus H. Darby, 1894), pp. 53–57.

Page 141: Samuel Bland Arnold, *Defense and Experience of a Lincoln Conspirator* (Hattiesburg, Miss., The Book Farm, 1943), pp. 18–19. This interesting compilation consists of Arnold's 1867 statement at Fort Jefferson and of his stories printed serially in New York and Baltimore newspapers (1902). He died in 1906.

Pages 141–142: Quoted in Clara E. Laughlin, *The Death of Lincoln* (New York, Doubleday, Page & Company, 1909), pp. 224–26. This was the first publication of the much advertised so-called Rockville lecture of John H. Surratt. Given in 1870, it was Surratt's first and last lecture. The speech is found also in *Lincoln Herald* (December, 1949).

Pages 142–143: Poore, *op. cit.,* pp. 71–72.

Pages 143–144: Arnold, *op. cit.,* pp. 21 and 45.

Pages 144–145: Laughlin, *op. cit.,* p. 228. It was not Chase.

Page 145: Pitman, *op. cit.,* p. 118. Weichmann's suspicions were reported to a co-worker, D. H. L. Gleason, who relayed them to his War Department superiors, but little came of it.

Page 146:
A. *Ibid.,* p. 99.
B. *Ibid.*
C. Booth's diary.
D. Quoted in Stanley Kimmel, *The Mad Booths of Maryland* (Indianapolis, The Bobbs-Merrill Company, 1940), p. 218.
E. Pitman, *op. cit.,* p. 113.

Page 147:
A. Poore, *op. cit.,* p. 189.
B. Nettie Mudd, *The Life of Dr. Samuel A. Mudd* (New York, Neale Publishing Company, 1906), p. 325.
C. Buckingham, *op. cit.,* p. 35.
D. F. L. Black, "How Lincoln Met Death," *Dearborn Independent* (May 28, 1925), p. 11.

Page 148:
A. Pitman, *op. cit.,* p. 74.
B. *Ibid.,* p. 72.

Pages 148–149: Buckingham, *op. cit.,* p. 13.

Page 149: John G. Nicolay and John Hay, "The Fourteenth of April," *Century Magazine* (January, 1890), p. 434. Major Rathbone, then twenty-eight, was a War Department attaché, with a distinguished war record; he had been brevetted three times. His widowed mother had married widower Senator Ira Harris of New York, father of Clara Harris. The two young persons were married in 1867. On December 23, 1883, while serving as U.S. consul in Hanover, Germany, Rathbone experienced a sudden maniacal seizure during which he was first frustrated in an attempt to shoot his children, but then shot and stabbed his wife to death and attempted suicide by stabbing. This horrendous incident led to a life sentence at the Hildersheim Hospital for the Criminal Insane, where he reportedly lived a life of ease until his death many years later in 1911.

Chapter VII

Page 152: Pitman, *op. cit.,* p. 79. Kimmel quotes a newspaper clipping in which Stewart is violently denounced as a humbug.

Page 153: *Ibid.,* p. 84.

Page 154: *Ibid.,* p. 85.

Pages 155–156: War Department Archives.

Page 157: War Department Records quoted in Theodore Roscoe, *Web of Conspiracy* (Englewood Cliffs, N. J., Prentice-Hall, 1959), p. 211.

Page 158: Thomas A. Jones, *J. Wilkes Booth* (Chicago, Laird & Lee, 1893), pp. 66 ff. Jones had served the Confederacy as a signal officer in lower Maryland. There is a story about him, probably apocryphal, of his being chased out of the Columbian Exposition by irate Union veterans to whom he had artlessly attempted to sell his book. The rare work was reprinted in *Amateur Collector* (September, October, November, 1954). The story of Booth's period of hiding was first made public in G. A. Townsend, "How Wilkes Booth Crossed the Potomac," *Century Magazine* (April, 1884).

Page 159: Booth's Diary. The mystery of Booth's diary is unfathomable. Taken from his body and delivered to Stanton it disappeared from sight. It came to light two years later when Colonel Baker's book was published. There has never been an explanation for the eighteen missing pages. It has been contended that had the defense known of it the diary would have tended to work in favor of Mrs. Surratt and Dr. Mudd. The bitter controversy concerning it is described in David Miller DeWitt, *The Assassination of Abraham Lincoln* (The Macmillan Company, 1909), and Eisenschiml, *Why Was Lincoln Murdered?* Presumably this diary entry was made several days after the assassination.

Pages 160–161: Jones, *op. cit.*

Page 162: Several writers have been misled by the date; Booth did not attempt a crossing Thursday night.

Pages 162–163: Jones, *op. cit.*, p. 111.

Page 163: Roscoe, *op. cit.*, p. 363.

Page 164: Pitman, *op. cit.*, p. 90.

Pages 164–165: M. B. Ruggles, "Pursuit and Death of John Wilkes Booth," *Century Magazine* (January, 1890), p. 444.

Page 165: F. L. Black, "The Pursuit and Capture of Booth," *Dearborn Independent* (April 11, 1925), p. 11. All those who aided Booth in his escape were arrested, ostensibly as accessories, and taken to Washington. Of the group only Dr. Mudd was prosecuted.

Chapter VIII

Page 166: Among the minor mysteries of the assassination aftermath is the one relating to the various versions of the reward posters. For instance, the poster used in this work shows photographs of the conspirators which were taken *after* their arrests. The enigma is explored in Roscoe, *op. cit.*

Page 168: General Lafayette C. Baker, *History of the United States Secret Service* (Philadelphia, L. C. Baker, 1867), p. 525. Openly denounced as a dictator, crook and humbug, Chief of the National Detective Police Lafayette C. Baker has in recent years acquired the stature of an arch-conspirator. Upon speculative evidence several present-day writers have accorded Colonel Baker the position of No. One Mystery Man of his day: Jacob Moglever, *Death to Traitors: The Story of General Lafayette C. Baker, Lincoln's Forgotten Secret Service Chief* (Doubleday, 1960); Robert H. Fowler, "Was Stanton Behind Lincoln's Murder?" *Civil War Times* (August-September, 1961); Vaughn Shelton, *Mask for Treason—The Lincoln Murder Trial* (Stackpole, 1965). Stanton's complicity in the President's death has never been established beyond the free-wheeling innuendoes popularized in Eisenschiml, *op. cit.*

Pages 168–169: Pitman, *op. cit.*, p. 87.

Page 169: Jones, *op. cit.*, pp. 69 ff.

Pages 170–171: Pitman, *op. cit.*, 122.

Page 171:
A. *Ibid.*, p. 123. Mrs. Surratt's alleged non-recognition of Payne was to weigh heavily against her. This evidence is disputed in David Miller, *The Assassination of Abraham Lincoln.*

B. *Ibid.*, p. 124.

Page 172: Ibid., p. 87.

Pages 172–174: Lieutenant Luther B. Baker, "An Eyewitness Account of the Death and Burial of J. Wilkes Booth," *Journal of the Illinois State Historical Society,* Vol. 29 (December, 1946), pp. 426 ff. Colonel Baker stated the source of his information as to Booth's whereabouts was "a colored man," who was never further identified and doubtless existed only in the Colonel's imagination. Most likely the information came from Major J. R. O'Beirne, who was denied permission to follow up on his lead.

Page 174:
A. A. R. Bainbridge, "Pursuit and Death of John Wilkes Booth," *Century Magazine* (January, 1890), p. 445.

B. William H. Garrett, "True Story of the Capture of John Wilkes Booth," *Confederate Veteran* (April, 1921), p. 129.

C. Monroe, *op. cit.*, p. 424.

Page 175: Pitman, *op. cit.*, p. 91.

Pages 175–177: Ibid. According to Eleanor Ruggles (*Prince of Players*), Edwin Booth reimbursed the Garretts for the loss of their barn.

Page 178: Lieut. L. B. Baker, *op. cit.*, p. 436.

Page 179:
A. Poore, *op. cit.*, p. 325; Pitman, *op. cit.*, pp. 94–95. It may well be conjectured that Booth shot himself and there is some evidence to substantiate the theory. Jones and Bainbridge quoted Booth as boasting he would never be taken alive and Herold stated Booth made a similar utterance while the barn was being surrounded. Moreover, the act of suicide was in keeping with the assassin's character. The theory is developed by Kimmel in *The Mad Booths of Maryland.*

B. Lieut. L. B. Baker, *op. cit.*, pp. 441 ff. Of the numerous accounts of the life of this religious fanatic the best is Lloyd Lewis, *Myths After Lincoln.* His post-war life is related in Albert T. Reid, "Boston Corbett," *Scribner's* (July, 1929).

Pages 180–181: Poore, *op. cit.*, pp. 316–18. Most tenacious of the assassination myths has been the legend of Booth's escape. The story has taken several forms but the principal one is that which had its genesis in Finis L. Bates, *The Escape and Suicide of John Wilkes Booth* (J. L. Nichols & Company, 1907), which unaccountably sold an estimated 75,000 copies. Others were believed to be the escaped Booth, and there have been the credulous who accepted the improbable tale. The fanciful tales of Bates and others are thoroughly discredited in George S. Bryan, *The Great American Myth* (Garrick & Evans, 1940). Bryan is equally devastating with the spurious claims of "Booth's" granddaughter, Izola Forrester, *This One Mad Act* (Hale, Cushman & Flint, 1937). A more recent study of the Oklahoma "Booth" of Bates is Mary Jo Banks, *The Enid Booth Legend* (Oklahoma Agriculture and Mechanics College, 1953). The myth is again pursued in Otto Eisenschiml, *In the Shadow of Lincoln's Death* (Wilfred Funk, 1940). Alva Johnson, "John Wilkes Booth on Tour," *Saturday Evening Post* (February 19, 1938), deals with the display of the mummified "Booth" of Bates' origin.

Page 182:
A. Lieut. L. B. Baker, *op. cit.*, pp. 441 ff. One of the pictures taken from Booth's body was that of Bessie Hale, daughter of Senator J. H. Hale of New Hampshire, and fiancée of the actor. Her identity was long kept secret. Some aspects of the betrothal are discussed in Asia Booth Clarke, *The Unlocked Book* (G. P. Putnam's Sons, 1938).

B. Oldroyd, *op. cit.*, p. 79.

Pages 182–183: Monroe, *loc. cit.*

Page 183: Pitman, *op. cit.,* p. 95. Basic reference for the positive identification of Booth's body is Dr. J. F. May, "Mark of the Scalpel," *Records of Columbia Historical Society,* 1910. Contrary to the myth-makers, the body was identified beyond doubt.

Page 184: Lieut. L. B. Baker, *op. cit.,* p. 444. The violently conflicting claims as to primacy among the leaders of the expedition were heard before several commissions and finally by Congress. As adjudicated the major award, $15,000, went to Conger, Colonel Baker received $3,750, Lieut. L. B. Baker, $3,000, Doherty, $5,250. Corbett's share was the same as that for the other troopers, $1,653.85. The total was $75,000. An additional $25,000 went to the captors of Atzerodt and $5,000 was paid for Payne's arrest.

Page 185: Frank Leslie's Illustrated Newspaper (May 20, 1865).

Chapter IX

Pages 188–189: Arnold, *op. cit.,* pp. 56–60.

Page 189: George Alfred Townsend, *op. cit.,* p. 62.

Page 190: R. A. Watts, "The Trial and Execution of the Lincoln Conspirators," *Michigan Magazine of History,* Vol. 5 (1922), p. 83.

Page 191:
A. *Harper's Weekly* (July 8, 1865).

B. Townsend, *op. cit.,* p. 64.

Page 192: Watts, *op. cit.,* p. 99.

Page 193:
A. William E. Doster, *Lincoln and Episodes of the Civil War* (New York, G. P. Putnam's Sons, 1915), pp. 260 ff. The dubious practice of trying civilians before a military tribunal in peacetime is discussed in John W. Curran, "Lincoln Conspiracy Trial and Military Jurisdiction over Civilians," *Notre Dame Lawyer* (November, 1933).

B. Watts, *op. cit.,* p. 91.

C. Noah Brooks, *Washington in Lincoln's Time* (New York, The Century Company, 1894), p. 272.

Page 194: Doster, *op. cit.,* p. 257.

Page 195:
A. "Benn Pitman Manuscripts," Tarbell-Lincoln Collection, Reis Library, Allegheny College. The Commission was not alone in its belief as to Confederate responsibility for the crime, the theory was held generally in the North. An aspect of this is treated in Seymour J. Frank, "The Conspiracy to Implicate the Confederate Leaders in Lincoln's Assassination," *Mississippi Valley Historical Review* (March, 1954).

B. Pratt, *op. cit.,* p. 139.

C. *Trial of the Alleged Assassins and Conspirators at Washington City, D. C., May and June, 1865* (Philadelphia, T. B. Peterson & Brothers, 1865), p. 16.

D. Brooks, *op. cit.,* p. 267. The actual measurements of the room were forty-five feet by twenty feet with an eleven foot ceiling.

Pages 196–197: Ibid., p. 268.

Page 198:
A. Pitman, *Assassination of the President . . .*, p. 97.

B. *Ibid.,* p. 98.

Page 199:
A. Nettie Mudd, *op. cit.,* p. 100.

B. T. M. Harris, *Assassination of Lincoln: A History of the Great Conspiracy* (Boston, American Citizen Company, 1892), p. 80. Although General Harris published his book twenty-seven years later, incredibly he still believed in the Confederate conspiracy and retained his inane phrenological theories.

C. Townsend, *op. cit.,* p. 68.

D. John W. Clampitt, "The Trial of Mrs. Surratt," *North American Review* (September, 1880), pp. 223 ff.

Page 200:
A. D. H. L. Gleason, "Conspiracy Against Lincoln," *Magazine of History* (February, 1911), p. 59. Washington street numbers had been changed when this story was written, hence the discrepancy of Mrs. Surratt's address with an earlier mention.

B. Clampitt, *loc. cit.* There are three book-length works dealing with the innocence of Mrs. Surratt. David Miller DeWitt, *The Judicial Murder of Mrs. Surratt* (John Murphy, 1895), and Guy W. Moore, *The Case of Mrs. Surratt* (University of Oklahoma Press, 1954), are both scholarly. A third work, Helen Jones Campbell, *The Case for Mrs. Surratt* (G. P. Putnam's Sons, 1943) is fictionalized. A three-act play by John Patrick, "The Story of Mary Surratt," appeared briefly in 1947.

Page 202: Henry Kyd Douglas, *I Rode with Stonewall* (Chapel Hill, University of North Carolina Press, 1940), p. 346. Annie Surratt was seventeen years old.

Page 203:
A. Doster, *op. cit.,* p. 265.

B. "Benn Pitman Manuscripts."

Pages 204–205: Clampitt, *loc. cit.* A protracted and bitter controversy between President Johnson and Judge Holt ended only when both were dead. Johnson stated flatly he had never seen the clemency plea for Mrs. Surratt and there is evidence that it was concealed from the President's eyes when he signed the death sentences. The two works of David Miller DeWitt elaborate on this much disputed question. The topic was being discussed in the periodicals as late as 1890.

Page 205: Doster, *op. cit.,* p. 279.

Pages 206–208: Townsend, *op. cit.,* pp. 70 ff.

Page 208:
A. Doster, *op. cit.,* p. 276.

B. John A. Gray, "Fate of the Lincoln Conspirators," *McClure's Magazine* (October, 1911), p. 636.

Page 212:
A. Doster, *op. cit.,* p. 278.

B. Watts, *op. cit.,* p. 108. John Surratt fled to Canada just before the assassination and remained there until September when he sailed for Rome where he became a Papal Zouave. Brought back to this country, apparently with government reluctance, he was tried June, 1867. After a sensational trial the jury failed to agree and he was later released. His strange adventures are related in Oldroyd, *op. cit.,* and in Eisenschiml, *In the Shadow of Lincoln's Death.*

C. Arnold, *op. cit.,* p. 63. Dr. Mudd, Arnold, O'Laughlin and Spangler were sent to the remote Fort Jefferson on Dry Tortugas in the Gulf of Mexico, an American Devil's Island. O'Laughlin died there during a virulent yellow-fever outbreak during which the doctor played a hero's part. Mudd, Arnold and Spangler were pardoned in February, 1869. The homeless Spangler came to the Mudd home where he remained until his death in 1881. The doctor passed away in January, 1883. The full story of the unfortunate doctor has been well told in Hal Higdon, *The Union vs. Dr. Mudd* (Follett, 1964). See also Nettie Mudd's account, *op. cit.*

BIBLIOGRAPHY

Many of the sources consulted are listed in the notes, and the reader with special interests may refer to them. For this reason the bibliography is a selective group of writings which are general in treatment, more readily available and in our judgment most meritorious in the area covered by the work.

BRYAN, GEORGE S., *The Great American Myth.* New York, Garrick & Evans, 1940. 436 pp.

EISENSCHIML, OTTO, *Why Was Lincoln Murdered?* New York, Little, Brown and Company, 1937. 503 pp.

KIMMEL, STANLEY, *The Mad Booths of Maryland.* Indianapolis, Bobbs-Merrill Company, 1940. 400 pp.

LEWIS, LLOYD, *Myths After Lincoln.* New York, Harcourt, Brace and Company, 1929. 367 pp.

MOORE, GUY W., *The Case of Mrs. Surratt.* Norman, University of Oklahoma Press, 1954. 142 pp.

ROSCOE, THEODORE, *The Web of Conspiracy: The Complete Story of the Men Who Murdered Abraham Lincoln.* Englewood Cliffs, Prentice-Hall, 1959. 562 pp.

SANDBURG, CARL, *Abraham Lincoln,* Vol. VI. New York, Harcourt, Brace and Company, 1939. 511 pp.

SEARCHER, VICTOR, *The Farewell to Lincoln.* New York, Abingdon Press, 1965. 320 pp.

INDEX